# CGP has Spanish translation cracked!

You can't make a Spanish omelette without breaking some eggs...
and you can't write a decent Spanish translation in the GCSE exams
without getting plenty of practice first.

That's why this brilliant CGP Workbook is the perfect way to prepare.
It's bursting with exercises that build up to exam-level translations — and
there's plenty of practice on all the key GCSE vocab and grammar too.

We've also included answers for every question, so you can be sure your
translations are on the right track. Everything you need for a top mark!

# CGP — still the best! ☺

Our sole aim here at CGP is to produce the highest quality books —
carefully written, immaculately presented and dangerously close to being funny.

Then we work our socks off to get them out to you
— at the cheapest possible prices.

# Contents

# Contents

Published by CGP

Editors:
Heather Cowley
Zoe Fenwick
Rose Jones
Gabrielle Richardson
Hannah Roscoe


Contributors:
Jennifer Akehurst
Abel and Anna Díaz
Jacqui Richards


With thanks to Chloe Anderson, Encarna Aparicio-Dominguez and Glenda Simpson for the proofreading.
With thanks to Ana Pungartnik for the copyright research.

ISBN: 978 1 78908051 3
Printed by Elanders Ltd, Newcastle upon Tyne.
Clipart from Corel®

Based on the classic CGP style created by Richard Parsons.

# The Translation Tasks

The translation tasks can seem daunting, but if you take them step-by-step, they'll look a lot less scary. Read through the texts and then tackle them sentence by sentence so that you can focus on each bit.

## The translation tasks are split over two exams

1) You'll need to translate <u>two short passages</u>, which will appear on different papers.

2) The <u>reading paper</u> will ask you to translate a short Spanish passage <u>into English</u>.

> See p.2-3 for more on translating into English and p.4-6 for translating into Spanish.

3) In the <u>writing paper</u>, you will have to translate a short English passage (or set of sentences) <u>into Spanish</u>.

## Keep an eye on the time

1) The translation question is likely to be one of the <u>last questions</u> on both the reading and writing exams. In both cases, it's worth <u>quite a few marks</u>, so make sure you <u>plan wisely</u> and leave <u>plenty of time</u> to answer it.

2) Remember you can tackle the exam questions in <u>any order</u> you choose, so you could start with the translation if you're <u>worried</u> about it. However, you might find it helpful to do the other reading and writing tasks first to <u>prepare</u> you for the translation and <u>remind</u> you of some of the words that you might need.

Jeremy couldn't believe he'd managed to lose track of the time.

## Read the translation carefully before you start

1) In both papers, make sure you read the <u>whole translation</u> carefully before you start writing — it's important to understand the <u>overall meaning</u> of the passage before starting to translate it.

2) Make yourself some <u>notes</u> before you start translating. Underline words or phrases that look <u>tricky</u> and jot down how you might <u>tackle</u> them.

3) Break up the translation into separate <u>sentences</u> rather than translating word-by-word. This will <u>avoid</u> any of the Spanish word order being <u>carried</u> into the English and vice versa.

4) <u>Don't panic</u> if you don't know a word or phrase — use the <u>context</u> to help you work it out. Be <u>creative</u> and think of another way to express it — it's important that your version has a <u>similar meaning</u> though.

5) You don't need to write a perfect translation first time — you can do it <u>roughly</u> first, and then write it up properly. Make sure you <u>cross out</u> old drafts with a <u>neat line</u>.

6) When you've finished, have a <u>fresh look</u> at every sentence, checking for <u>verb tenses</u>, <u>word order</u> and that you haven't <u>missed out</u> any words or sentences from the translation.

---

### *El tiempo se me escapó — time got away from me...*

It's really important to give yourself enough time to check over your answer once you've done your translation. Think about what your weak points are and keep them in mind when you're looking out for any little mistakes.

---

# Translating Spanish into English

Translating into English is usually easier than into Spanish, because you're more familiar with the sentence structure. You still need to make sure your English sounds as natural as possible though.

## First read the whole text to get the gist

1) As you read the text, you should be able to spot some words that you <u>already know</u>. Once you've got the gist, if there are any words you don't know, the <u>context</u> of the text can help you to <u>work them out</u>.

2) If you're stuck, you can try to <u>guess</u> some Spanish words that look or sound the <u>same as English</u> words, e.g. delicioso — *delicious*, celebración — *celebration*, vocabulario — *vocabulary*.

3) Be careful though — you might come across a '<u>false friend</u>'. This is a Spanish word that looks like an English word, but has a <u>completely different meaning</u>:

| | | | | | | | | | | |
|---|---|---|---|---|---|---|---|---|---|---|
| la nota | *mark* | la carpeta | *folder, file* | la arena | *sand* | la librería | *bookshop* | actual | *present* |
| el pie | *foot* | la dirección | *address* | el éxito | *success* | sensible | *sensitive* | educado | *polite* |
| gracioso | *funny* | el pariente | *relative* | la ropa | *clothes* | el campo | *countryside* | mayor | *older* |

## You'll have to change the word order in English

1) As you translate <u>each sentence</u>, you'll need to look carefully at the <u>word order</u>.

2) <u>Adjectives</u> often come after the noun in Spanish sentences, so remember to check the order is correct in English:

> Compré la **manzana roja**.　*I bought the **apple red**.* ✖　*I bought the **red apple**.* ✓

3) <u>Adverbs</u> sometimes appear in a different <u>order</u> in Spanish and English sentences. You'll need to think about how to make your translation sound <u>natural</u>:

> **Siempre** juego al rugby.　***Always** I play rugby.* ✖　*I **always** play rugby.* ✓

4) Think carefully about whether you need to use an <u>article</u> in English:

> Me encanta **la** historia.　*I love **the** history.* ✖　*I love history.* ✓

> Soy profesora.　*I am teacher.* ✖　*I am **a** teacher.* ✓ ← Spanish doesn't need an article with job statements like this — don't forget to add it in English.

## You need to translate some proper nouns

*Proper nouns are nouns that refer to a specific person or place, e.g. 'John' or 'Spain'.*

1) You don't need to translate <u>people's names</u>, e.g. 'Tomás'.

2) You will need to translate any <u>place names</u> that are written differently in English, e.g. Sudamérica — *South America*, España — *Spain*, el Reino Unido — *the United Kingdom*.

3) You will also need to translate the names of some festivals and celebrations, e.g. Navidad — *Christmas*, la Nochevieja — *New Year's Eve*, la Pascua — *Easter*.

# Translating Spanish into English

## Be careful when translating verbs

1) The exam translation will contain a <u>variety</u> of tenses. As you translate each verb, think about <u>who</u> or <u>what</u> is doing the action and <u>which tense</u> you need in English.

2) Think carefully when translating <u>verbs in the infinitive</u> — they are sometimes translated as '-ing' verbs in English.

> Mañana tengo que **ir** al ayuntamiento. ➡ *Tomorrow I have **to go** to the town hall.*
>
> Tengo muchas ganas de **ver** el palacio. ➡ *I'm looking forward to **seeing** the palace.*

3) Many verbs in Spanish are <u>identical</u> in the 'nosotros' form of the <u>preterite and present tense</u>. You'll need to use the <u>context</u> of the extract and clues about when the action <u>took place</u> to help you decide which tense to use in English.

> Ayer **jugamos** al baloncesto. ➡ *Yesterday we **played** basketball.*
>
> Siempre **jugamos** al baloncesto. ➡ *We always **play** basketball.*

## Remember to check your answer

1) Once you've finished, <u>reread</u> your answer to make sure it sounds like something you'd say in English. It's important to <u>leave time</u> to do this, as there will almost always be some <u>mistakes</u>.

Counting the mistakes in Fred's translation was about as fun as counting sheep.

2) Read through your translation to make sure it sounds <u>natural</u>. Some words and phrases don't translate <u>literally</u>, so you'll need to make sure your sentences sound <u>right</u> in English.

> Irene **hizo** su maleta.   *Irene **made** her suitcase.* ✖   *Irene **packed** her suitcase.* ✓

> Voy a **tomar** un café.   *I'm going to **take** a coffee.* ✖   *I'm going to **have** a coffee.* ✓

3) Keep an eye out for <u>set phrases</u> — you'll need to just <u>remember</u> how to translate these:

> Te echo de menos. ➡ *I miss you.*   ⟵ This phrase doesn't make sense when translated literally from Spanish.

4) See if anything unusual <u>stands out</u> when reading it back in English. You might have translated a phrase <u>one way</u> but it could sound <u>out of place</u> in the context of the passage <u>as a whole</u>.

---

### 'Los pies' — not as 'deliciosos' as they sound...

Translating into English isn't so bad — you can speak the language after all. Just watch out for some of the things that don't translate very smoothly from Spanish. When you've finished, make sure your translation still makes sense in English.

# Translating English into Spanish

The most important thing when translating into Spanish is to make sure you have translated the meaning of everything in the English text — even if Spanish uses a different number of words.

## Read the whole passage through first

1) When you first read the text, you might come across a <u>phrase</u> or <u>sentence</u> you can't translate literally into Spanish. If so, it might be because it's not <u>expressed</u> in the same way in English.

2) If you don't know how to translate a phrase, think of the <u>simplest way</u> you know how to write the sentence in Spanish — just make sure you've got across the <u>meaning</u> of the English passage.

3) If there's a word you don't know how to translate, find a <u>synonym</u> in English. For example, if you are asked to translate 'I often play football', and don't know the Spanish for '<u>often</u>', you could use the word '<u>usually</u>' instead, e.g: 'Normalmente juego al fútbol'.

4) It's hard to write '<u>natural</u>' Spanish when it's not your native language. Try to work as accurately as possible. You can use the <u>checklist</u> on p.6 to help you.

## Be careful translating verbs into Spanish

1) Before you start translating, look at the <u>English verbs</u> and jot down the <u>tenses</u> you'll need to use to translate them into Spanish.

2) Make sure you know which English verbs are translated using <u>reflexive verbs</u> in Spanish. Underline any in the text so you don't forget the <u>reflexive pronoun</u> when translating.

> He **gets up** at 8 o'clock. → **Se levanta** a las ocho.
>
> I am going **to stay** in a hotel. → Voy a **quedarme** en un hotel.

3) Watch out for impersonal verbs like 'doler' and 'gustar' — you'll need to make sure that the verb agrees with the noun and not the person.

> My eyes hurt. → Me duel**en los** ojos.

> They like cheese. → Les gusta **el** queso.

## Make sure you choose the correct verb

1) Think carefully about the verb you will need to use when translating into Spanish — it may be expressed using a <u>different verb</u> to English:

> I **take** photos. → **Saco** fotos.

In Spanish, you can't use the verb 'tomar' (to take) when talking about photos. You need to use 'sacar' for this.

2) Watch out for translating the verb '<u>to be</u>'. You can use '<u>ser</u>' or '<u>estar</u>' (see p.5), but in some contexts, you'll need a <u>different verb</u> in Spanish:

> He **is** scared. → *Él* **tiene** miedo.

> It **is** cold. → **Hace** frío.

# Translating English into Spanish

## Think about the order of object pronouns

1) In Spanish, object pronouns normally come <u>before</u> the verb:

> Ricardo saw **it**. → *Ricardo **lo** vio.*

2) For <u>commands</u>, the pronoun <u>is added to the end</u> of the verb. This also happens when the verb is written in the <u>infinitive</u>:

> Write to **me**. → *Escríbe**me**.*

> I want to see **it**. → *Quiero ver**lo**.*

## Make sure your adjectives agree

1) In Spanish, adjectives need to <u>agree</u> with the <u>noun</u> they describe. Think carefully about whether the noun is <u>masculine</u> or <u>feminine</u>, <u>singular</u> or <u>plural</u>.

> The fish is very tasty. → ***El** pescado está muy ric**o**.*
>
> The beaches are beautiful. → ***Las** playas son bonit**as**.*

2) Remember to think about <u>word order</u> when translating adjectives. Most adjectives come <u>after</u> the word they describe, but some adjectives <u>change their meaning</u> depending on their position.

> A **long-standing** friend → *Un **viejo** amigo*
>
> An **elderly** friend → *Un amigo **viejo***

Tempers were running high after John accidentally called Bob his 'elderly friend'.

## Choose your words carefully

1) Spanish sometimes uses different words for different situations, where the <u>same word</u> would be used in English.

2) 'Por' and 'para' both mean 'for', but they're each used in <u>different circumstances</u>:

> This money is **for** you. → *Este dinero es **para** ti.*
>
> I paid two euros **for** the tea. → *Pagué dos euros **por** el té.*

3) 'Ser' and 'estar' are both forms of 'to be' in Spanish, but they're used for <u>different situations</u>:

> **You are** very kind. → ***Eres** muy amable.*
>
> **You are** sad today. → ***Estás** triste hoy.*

The first sentence uses 'ser' because it is talking about a general characteristic. The second sentence describes a temporary feeling, so it uses 'estar'.

# Translating English into Spanish

## Accents are an important part of word meaning

1) Think carefully about when to use accents as they can <u>change the meaning</u> of a word, e.g. yes — *sí*, if — *si*.

2) Make sure you pay attention to the accents on verbs in different tenses — they can <u>change</u> the <u>tense</u> and <u>subject</u> of the verb:

> **He bought** a new bag. ➔ *Compró una bolsa nueva.*
>
> **I buy** a new bag. ➔ *Compro una bolsa nueva.*

John couldn't understand why no one was excited by his offer to play a couple more songs.

3) Some words <u>lose</u> their accents in their <u>plural</u> form, e.g. song — *la canción*, songs — *las canciones*.

4) Remember to <u>add</u> an accent to the <u>interrogatives</u> when you're asking a <u>question</u>, e.g. Where are you from? — ¿De dónde eres?

Remember to use upside-down question marks when writing questions in Spanish.

## Check through your work thoroughly

1) Once you've done your Spanish translation, <u>go back</u> through it and check that you've covered <u>everything</u> that was in the English. It's easy to miss out <u>little words</u> like 'very' or 'always'.

2) This <u>checklist</u> is a handy reminder of the kinds of things you should look out for when reading through your work. Learn <u>these points</u> and keep them in mind as you <u>check</u> your translation.

> * Are all the <u>verbs</u> in the <u>right tense</u>?
>   *Ayer juego al fútbol.* ✘          *Ayer jugué al fútbol.* ✓
>
> * Are the <u>verb endings</u> correct?
>   *Me duele los brazos.* ✘          *Me duelen los brazos.* ✓
>
> * Do your <u>adjectives agree</u> with their nouns?
>   *La camisa es amarillo.* ✘          *La camisa es amarilla.* ✓
>
> * Are your <u>adjectives</u> in the <u>right place</u>?
>   *Una blanca falda.* ✘          *Una falda blanca.* ✓
>
> * Do your <u>reflexive pronouns</u> and <u>reflexive verb endings</u> agree?
>   *A las siete, me levantamos.* ✘          *A las siete, me levanto.* ✓
>
> * Have you spelt everything correctly, including using the right accents?
>   *El toca la guitar con su tio.* ✘          *Él toca la guitarra con su tío.* ✓

---

### *With everything on these pages, you'll be prepared for éxito...*

You might feel under pressure in the exam, but it's really important that you don't rush — that's when you're bound to make mistakes. Leave time to check your work at the end and make sure you've translated every part of the text.

# About Yourself

**Q1** Translate these sentences into **English**. Before you start, <u>underline</u> the verb or verbs in each sentence. The first one has been done for you.

a)  <u>Me llamo</u> Ana Luisa.

b)  Mi amigo tiene catorce años.

c)  El cumpleaños de Luca es el veinte de mayo.

d)  No sé cómo escribir tu apellido.

**Q2** Translate the phrases in bold into **Spanish**. The first one has been done for you. Then translate each sentence — you'll need the 'we' form for each one.

a)  **My brother and I are** Spanish. ▷ ....**Mi hermano y yo somos**....

b)  **Paul and I are** thirteen years old. ▷ ..............................................

c)  **We live** in a city which is called Pamplona. ▷ ..............................................

d)  **We celebrated** his third birthday yesterday. ▷ ..............................................

**Q3** Translate these questions into **Spanish**. Use the 'tú' form of the verb.

a)  What are you called?

b)  Are you from the north of Spain?

c)  When is your birthday?

d)  Where do you live?

> Remember you need an upside-down question mark at the start of each of your Spanish questions.

**Q4** Translate the following passage into **Spanish**.

> Which tense do you need to say what someone 'used to' do?

My name is Yusef and I am sixteen. <u>We used to live</u> in Madrid, but now we live in Alicante. My brother is called Khaled. We are twins! Our birthday is <u>the 28th of July</u>.

> Have a look back at Q1 for a reminder of how to write dates in Spanish.

**Q5** Translate the following passage into **English**.

Mi mejor amiga se llama Coral, pero la mayoría del tiempo la llamamos Cori. Su fecha de nacimiento es el treinta de marzo de 2004, así que su cumpleaños cae el día después del mío. Cori es de nacionalidad peruana.

When you've finished, check:

☐ Verbs — have you used the right 'person' of the verb?

☐ Word order — does it sound like natural English? If not, can you fix it by changing the word order?

 ☐  ☐  ☐

# My Family

**Q1**  Complete the Spanish sentences with the present tense 'they' form of the verb in brackets. Then translate the sentences into **English**.

a)  Cada viernes Zara y Dani ............**van**............ al cine con mi hermanastra.  **(ir)**

b)  Tengo unos parientes que ........................ en Gales.  **(vivir)**

c)  Los primos de Rita ........................ Jorge y Flora.  **(llamarse)**

d)  Mis tíos ........................ unos hijos adoptados.  **(tener)**

**Q2**  Translate these sentences into **Spanish**. Before you start, underline the plural nouns. The first one has been done for you.

a)  My older <u>sisters</u> don't live with us.

b)  Leah's stepfather has three daughters.

c)  Do you know my nephews?

d)  My wife doesn't have brothers or sisters.

**Q3**  Translate this passage into **Spanish**.
Before you start, answer the questions below.

> Look back at Q1 for a clue on how to say 'cousins'.

> I am an only child but I spend a lot of time with my <u>cousins</u>.
> Last week, my uncle got married, so my cousins have a stepmother.
> She is called Lili and the most important thing is that she is friendly.

*When one of the guests criticised her dress, Lili really took a fence.*

a)  What's 'only child' in Spanish? ................................................

b)  Which tenses will you need for the second sentence? ................................................

c)  How will you translate 'the most important thing'? ................................................

**Q4**  Traduce el texto siguiente al **inglés**.

> Look at the rest of the sentence to help you translate 'cuyos'.

> A mis abuelos les gusta sentarse en el parque y escuchar a los niños que juegan allí. Ayer vieron a un hombre <u>cuyos</u> hijos pequeños estaban saludando a todo el mundo de manera muy graciosa. Cuando sea mayor, <u>me encantaría</u> tener hijos como ellos.

> Which tense is this?

When you've finished, check:

☐ Tenses — have you thought carefully about which to use?

☐ Adjectives — are they in the right place in the sentence?

# Describing People

**Q1** Translate these sentences into **Spanish**. Before you start, circle the adjective or adjectives in each sentence. The first one has been done for you.

a) Carlos has (green) eyes.

b) José Luis has straight hair.

c) Nancy is quite slim.

d) They have short, blonde hair.

e) I wear glasses. They are black.

f) Lisa and I have long, curly hair.

*Remember — most of the time, Spanish adjectives come after the noun they describe.*

**Q2** Translate the comparisons in bold into **English**. Then translate the whole sentence. The first comparison has been done for you.

a) Paula es **más alta que** Erica. ▷ ..........taller than..........

b) Eres **mucho más joven que** tu primo. ▷ ..........................................

c) Yo soy **tan guapo como** Dan. ▷ ..........................................

d) Annabel **no es tan fuerte como** mi hermanastra. ▷ ..........................................

**Q3** Complete the Spanish sentences with the correct imperfect tense form of the verb in brackets. The first one has been done for you. Then translate the sentences into **English**.

a) Felipe ..........tenía.......... el pelo más largo que yo.                    (tener)

b) June y Neil ..................... gafas de plástico.                    (llevar)

c) Yo ..................... muy baja, pero ahora soy bastante alta.                    (ser)

d) Mi hermana siempre ..................... un piercing.                    (querer)

**Q4** Marisa works in an optician's and is recommending some glasses to Nick. Translate their dialogue into **Spanish**.

*As Marisa and Nick don't know each other, they'll both need to use the formal 'you'.*

a) **Marisa:** We have these blue glasses. Do you like them?
   **Nick:** I think they are too big. I have quite a small face.

b) **Marisa:** If you're looking for smaller glasses, we have these red ones.
   **Nick:** No, I'm red-haired, so I would prefer to have a different colour.

c) **Marisa:** We also sell brown glasses. Lots of young people wear glasses like <u>these</u>.
   **Nick:** I love those! Thank you for your help.

'These' needs to agree with the object it's describing.

# Personalities

**Q1** Translate these sentences containing adverbs into **English**.

a) A veces mi prima es comprensiva.

b) Izzy siempre es animada y nunca es perezosa.

c) De vez en cuando, mi hermano menor es tímido.

d) Mi mejor amigo es hablador y siempre gracioso.

*Think about the position of the adverb in the sentence when you translate these.*

**Q2** Complete the sentences by translating the adjective in brackets into Spanish. The first one has been done for you. Then translate the sentences into **English**.

a) Un buen amigo es ............**generoso**............ . **(generous)**

b) Mis enemigos son muy ................................ . **(unpleasant)**

c) Olivia y Carla parecen ................................ . **(hard-working)**

d) Vuestra madre suele ser ................................ . **(friendly)**

*Make sure the adjectives agree with the nouns in each sentence.*

**Q3** Translate the sentences below into **Spanish**, thinking carefully about the negatives.

a) I wasn't brave when I was little.

b) Nerea and Ana will never be honest.

c) There is no one as <u>lazy</u> as you.

d) Philip isn't chatty any more.

*Look at Q1 for a clue on how to translate 'lazy'.*

**Q4** Saskia has written a note to Eva to apologise for her behaviour. Translate her message into **Spanish**.

*Use the verb 'intentar' for 'to try'.*

Hi Eva. I know that I am sometimes selfish. I will <u>try</u> to be more generous in the future and will always share my sweets <u>with you</u>. I'm really sorry. Saskia.

*How will you translate 'with you'?*

**Q5** Translate this passage into **English**.

Mi novio ideal sería creativo y activo. Una característica que no puedo aguantar* es la arrogancia. Mi novio ideal sería alguien que no piense que sea la persona más importante del mundo. Además, me gustaría salir con alguien que tenga un buen sentido del humor y que me haga reír.

*aguantar = to stand (something)

Before you start, check:

☐ Vocabulary — do you know it all? If there's a word you don't know, can you guess it?

☐ Tenses — think about which tenses you need in each of the sentences.

Section 2 — Me, My Family and Friends

# Pets

**Q1** Translate the underlined adjectives into **Spanish**. Then translate the sentences, making sure the adjectives agree with the nouns.

a) My dog has <u>brown</u> eyes.

b) I have two <u>white</u> rabbits.

c) My grandparents' tortoise is very <u>old</u>.

d) Normally, my cat is <u>affectionate</u>.

e) My friend has <u>many</u> goldfish.

f) Our guinea pigs are <u>funny</u>.

**Q2** Translate these sentences into **English**. Before you start, note down which tense is used for the verbs in bold.

a) **Me gustaría** tener un gato gris.

b) **Tenía** dos caballos que **se llamaban** Fred y Louis.

c) **Fui** a un acuario con mi primo y **vimos** peces tropicales.

d) En el futuro, **compraré** un perro grande.

e) Mi amigo **tiene** un conejillo de Indias.

f) El conejo de mi hermana **ha comido** todas las lechugas en el jardín.

Fred and Louis were pretty similar, but one would always be just a little more hoarse...

**Q3** In Spanish, you can add suffixes to nouns and adjectives to change their meaning slightly. Translate the bold words into **English**. The first one has been done for you. Then translate the whole sentence.

a) Mi **gatito** es muy inteligente. ➡ ..........little cat..........

b) Tengo un perro **pequeñito** que se llama Iggie. ➡ ..........................................

c) Mi hámster era **gordísimo**. ➡ ..........................................

d) Para mí, es **importantísimo** tener una mascota. ➡ ..........................................

**Q4** Translate this passage into **Spanish**.

My brother wants a pet, so I am going to buy him a rabbit. The rabbit is three months old and is black and white. It has a pink nose and <u>really long</u> ears. It's a very pretty animal. It will have a <u>little house</u> in our garden.

Use a suffix for these. Have a look back at Q3.

When you've finished, check:

☐ Adjective agreements — do all the adjectives agree with the nouns?

☐ Verbs — have you used the right 'person' of the verb?

# Style and Fashion

**Q1** Translate these questions into **English**. Before you start, think about how to translate the underlined question words.

a) ¿<u>De quién</u> es esta gorra negra?

b) ¿<u>Cuál</u> prefieres, esta blusa azul o aquella blusa de rayas?

c) ¿<u>Con quién</u> compraste esta falda?

*Think carefully about your word order when you translate these into English.*

**Q2** Use the correct form of either 'gustar' or 'encantar' to translate these sentences into **Spanish**.

a) I like your bracelet.

b) They love my tie.

c) Silvia loves <u>leather jackets</u>.

d) Dimitri would like a <u>cotton shirt</u>.

*In Spanish, you say 'jackets of leather' and 'shirt of cotton'.*

**Q3** Complete the Spanish sentences with the correct future tense form of the verb in brackets. The first one has been done for you. Then translate the sentences into **English**.

a) Tania ......**comprará**...... un suéter en vez de una camiseta.          **(comprar)**

b) El año que viene, nosotros no ......................... que llevar uniforme.          **(tener)**

c) Si hace frío, pienso que yo ......................... una bufanda de lana.          **(llevar)**

d) Aquellos pantalones te ......................... bien.          **(quedar)**

**Q4** Translate the following passage into **Spanish**. Before you start, look at the verbs in bold — they'll all be in the infinitive form in the Spanish version.

> For me, **being** fashionable isn't important. It is more important **to choose** comfortable clothes. In the summer, I like **wearing** shorts <u>instead of</u> jeans.

*Look at Q3 for a clue on how to say 'instead of'.*

**Q5** Traduce el texto siguiente al **inglés**.

> Los jóvenes hoy en día tienen estilos muy distintos. Algunos tienen un estilo alternativo con tatuajes <u>mientras que</u> otros tienen un estilo más formal. En mi opinión, es importante estar en la onda <u>y</u> vestirme bien. Pienso que todo el mundo llevará ropa de materiales reciclados <u>cuando</u> sea mayor.

When you've finished, check:

☐ Word order — does your English 'flow'? Look at the first sentence in particular.

☐ Conjunctions — have you translated the underlined phrases accurately?

# Relationships

**Q1** Translate the following sentences into **English**. Before you start, underline the reflexive verbs. The first verb has been underlined for you.

a) <u>Me llevo</u> bien con mi hermana menor.

b) Nos enamoramos hace un año.

c) Siempre me siento relajado con ella.

d) Me divierto pasando tiempo con mis amigos.

e) Suelo relacionarme bien con otra gente.

f) A veces mi hermano y yo nos peleamos.

**Q2** Translate the phrases in bold into **Spanish**. The first one has been done for you. Then translate the whole sentence. You'll need the imperfect tense for all of these.

a) My siblings and I **used to fight** a lot. ⟹ ........... nos peleábamos ...........

b) Tula and I **used to have** a good relationship. ⟹ ...............................................

c) My dad and I **used to get on** well. ⟹ ...............................................

d) My cousins always **annoyed me**. ⟹ ...............................................

You'll need to use the personal 'a' in this sentence after the verb.

e) I **didn't used to know** my uncle. ⟹ ...............................................

**Q3** Translate this passage into **Spanish**. Before you start, read the tips and answer the questions.

Every Monday, I visit my grandmother. We get on very well and she <u>supports</u> me when I have arguments with my friends. She would never <u>judge</u> me, but it annoys her a lot when I talk while <u>I'm eating</u>.

How will you translate this into Spanish?

You'll need the verb 'juzgar' here.

If 'el apoyo' means 'support', how will you translate this?

**Q4** Translate these conversations into **English**. Try to make your English sound as natural as possible.

a) **Miguel:** ¿Te llevas bien con tus hermanos, Tania?
   **Tania:** Cuando era más pequeña, no, pero ahora sí.

b) **Adrián:** ¿Conoces bien a tu sobrino, Mónica?
   **Mónica:** No, desafortunadamente no nos conocemos muy bien.

c) **Pilar:** ¿Cómo van las cosas con tu novio, Rosa?
   **Rosa:** Todo va bien. Confío en él y pienso que me he enamorado de él de verdad.

Tania thought she and her siblings had a great relationship — until they burst her bubble...

# Socialising with Friends and Family

**Q1** Translate these sentences into **English**. Before you start, think carefully about the meaning of 'que' in each example.

**a)** ¿**Qué** vas a hacer este fin de semana, Tamal?

**b)** Tengo muchos parientes **que** viven cerca de mí.

**c)** Raúl, ¿tienes el regalo **que** compramos para Pedro?

**d)** Iré a un restaurante con mi familia, **lo que** será divertido.

**Q2** Translate these opinions into **Spanish**. Think carefully about how to translate the expressions in bold — will you need an infinitive or a continuous form?

**a)** **Alana:** I like **spending time** with my sisters when they're in a good mood.

**b)** **Clara:** I hate it when I'm **studying** and my brother is **playing** with his friends.

**c)** **Maxi:** It's impossible to talk to my parents while they're **cooking**.

**d)** **Resul:** Well, I prefer **going out** with my friends. If I stay at home, I have to babysit.

**e)** **Luna:** My cousins are naughty, so I don't like **sharing** my things with them.

**Q3** Complete the sentences using the preterite tense of the verbs in brackets. The first one has been done for you. Then translate the sentences into **English**.

**a)** Ayer ..........**fui**.......... al parque temático con mis amigos.  **(ir)**

**b)** Yo no ...................... con Rafael porque era engreído y mimado.  **(hablar)**

**c)** ...................... la película una vez con mi tía y otra vez con mi amigo.  **(ver)**

**d)** Mi padre ...................... a los niños cómo jugar al tenis.  **(enseñar)**

**e)** Mi amiga me ...................... porque ella quería consejos.  **(llamar)**

**Q4** Translate this passage into **Spanish**.

> You'll need to use 'que' in this phrase.

My best friend is called Paco. Our friendship is very important to me and he is the <u>most loyal person I know</u>. For example, when other people in our gang bullied me last year, he supported me. We love travelling together, so next year we will go to Portugal.

When you've finished, check:

☐ Pronouns — have you translated these correctly?

☐ Verbs — have you chosen the correct verbs for your translation?

 ☐  ☐  ☐

# Partnership

**Q1** Translate the infinitives in bold into **English**. Then translate the whole sentence. The first one has been done for you.

a) Espero **casarme** con un hombre simpático. ➡️ .............**to get married**.............

b) Me gustaría **enamorarme** en el futuro. ➡️ ......................................

c) Tengo la intención de **tener** al menos un hijo. ➡️ ......................................

d) Quiero una fiesta grande para **celebrar** mi casamiento. ➡️ ......................................

**Q2** Translate these sentences into **Spanish**. Before you start, think about which tense you'll need to use for the verb or verbs in each sentence.

a) My uncle married his neighbour.

b) He met someone a few weeks ago.

c) My grandparents recently separated.

d) His friends got engaged at the weekend.

e) I don't want to get married because I like being single.

This wasn't what Polly had envisaged when she asked Feathers for a cracker...

**Q3** After a few months of thinking about their relationship, Violeta has decided to have an important conversation with Diego. Translate their dialogue into **English**.

a) **Violeta:** Diego, el día en que nos conocimos, decidí que quería pasar el resto de mi vida contigo. Eres la persona que más quiero en el mundo y por eso quiero que nos casemos. ¿Qué piensas?

b) **Diego:** ¿En serio? ¡Sería fantástico! <u>Siempre nos hemos llevado bien</u> y somos un equipo fenomenal. ¡No puedo esperar!

The word order will be different in English.

**Q4** Traduce el texto siguiente al **español**.

Can you think of another way to say this in English?

My parents <u>have been married</u> for 15 years. It seems like they have a happy marriage because they laugh when they are together and they <u>hardly ever</u> fight. I hope to get married one day, but my mum has advised that <u>I finish</u> my studies first.

Which verb and tense will you need here?

You'll need the subjunctive for this verb.

# Mixed Practice

**Q1**   Translate these sentences into **English**.

**a)**   Gracias por invitarme a tu casamiento.  Me encantaría asistir.

**b)**   Te invito a mi fiesta de cumpleaños el martes que viene.

**c)**   <u>Lamento</u> oír que tus padres han decidido separarse.  ⟵   *Tip — 'lamento' means the same as 'lo siento'.*

**d)**   Felicitaciones por tu boda.  Te deseo todo lo mejor en este día especial.

**e)**   ¿Es verdad que queréis <u>divorciaros</u>?  Siempre parecíais felices juntos.

*Watch out — this looks like a plural noun, but it's a verb with a pronoun.*

**Q2**   Traduce el texto siguiente al **inglés**.

> A Iratxe siempre le han gustado los gatos.  Recientemente, ha adoptado un gato pequeño de color gris y blanco que se llama Toby.  Es muy animado, ¡pero es muy torpe!  La semana pasada, rompió unos vasos en el comedor.  Lo bueno es que a Iratxe no le importa, porque quiere a Toby mucho.

*After finding out that his 'surprise party' was actually a family reunion, Mr Mittens was ready for revenge.*

**Q3**   Translate this text into **Spanish**.

> My name is Oscar.  When I was little, I was a bit mischievous, but I wasn't lazy or selfish.  Now I think I am quite reserved.  My best friend, Marco, is very polite and he's more serious than me.  Next year, we will go to different schools.

**Q4**   Translate this conversation into **Spanish**.

**Father:**  What do you want for your birthday?

**Son:**     I would like to have a dog.  I would walk it every day and would play with it in the garden.

**Father:**  A dog is a big responsibility.  Who would look after it when you're at school?  We couldn't leave it in the house all day <u>by itself</u>.

**Son:**     I don't know.  Maybe it would be better to have a goldfish.   *Can you think of a different way of saying this in English?*

# Mixed Practice

**Q5**   Translate these sentences into **Spanish**.

**a)**   I can't bear my brother's girlfriend.
She's very greedy and rude.

**b)**   Her wife is medium height.
She has green eyes.

**c)**   She got engaged to a slim man
with long, chestnut-brown hair.

**d)**   Roberto's nephew is very young.
He'll be two years old next January.

**e)**   My stepsister is very chatty.
She never stops talking!

**f)**   Mika's cousin was jealous of
his relationship with Danilo.

**Q6**   Translate this text into **English**.

> Mi hermana escribe un blog sobre la moda. Ella tiene
> un estilo retro y lleva ropa pasada de moda. Ayer se
> puso una chaqueta de cuero <u>agujereada</u>. Cuando sea
> adulta, le gustaría ser escritora para una revista de moda.
> Personalmente, me gusta llevar ropa más moderna.

*If the noun 'agujero'
means 'hole', what
do you think
'agujereada' means?*

**Q7**   Traduce las frases siguientes al **español**.

**a)**   Leila is my twin. She used to have long hair, but now she has short hair.
Her fiancé is generous and friendly. I get on really well with him.

**b)**   My father's youngest brother is medium height. He's bald and wears glasses.
He has a black dog called Hugo, which is usually well behaved.

**c)**   Last week, our grandparents looked after us. We argued a lot because
they thought we didn't behave well and that we were too <u>immature</u>.

*If 'maduro' means 'mature',
can you guess how you'd
say 'immature' in Spanish?*

**d)**   My aunt is very understanding. When I have a problem, she
always gives me good advice. I trust her a lot.

**Q8**   Traduce el texto siguiente al **español**.

> My cousin is called Andrés and he was born on the 23rd of April, the
> same day as me! Every year, we celebrate our birthdays together. This
> year, Andrés wants to go to the bowling alley with some friends, but I'd
> prefer to go to a restaurant. With luck, we will be able to do both things.

# Mixed Practice

**Q9**   Lola e Ibón están hablando de sus familias.  Traduce la conversación al **inglés**.

**Lola:**   Soy hija única.  Me gustaría tener hermanos, pero mis padres
no quieren tener más hijos.  ¿Tienes hermanos, Ibón?

**Ibón:**   Sí, tengo un hermano.  Me parezco mucho a él, aunque tiene el pelo más
largo que yo.  Mis padres quieren que se corte el pelo, pero él no quiere.

**Lola:**   A mi hermano, no le importa la moda.  ¿Cómo es tu hermano?

**Ibón:**   Es una persona muy independiente.  Nunca lleva ropa de marca tampoco.

**Q10**   Translate these sentences into **Spanish**.

**a)**   My ideal boyfriend would be friendly and intelligent.  He'd have
dark hair and blue eyes.  We'd be interested in the same things.

**b)**   I would spend my ideal birthday with my family.  A few years
ago, I went to the zoo with my nieces and we had a great time.

**c)**   Rico's best friend is called Sophia.  They love going for walks in
the park and playing together.  She was very shy when I met her,
but now she's more talkative.

*Jaime never understood why Julia
didn't want a second date...*

**Q11**   Snow White has posted this message on an advice forum.  Translate it into **English**.

Hola, me llamo Blancanieves*.  Mi vida familiar siempre ha sido difícil.  Hace dos
años mi padre murió, dejándome con mi madrastra.  Ella está celosa de mí, sobre
todo del pelo negro que tengo.  Me gustaría mejorar la relación entre nosotras,
pero ella pasa todo el tiempo en su habitación hablando con su reflejo feísimo.

*Blancanieves = Snow White

**Q12**   You see this advert for a pet sitter in a magazine.  Translate it into **English**.

¿Usted busca a alguien para cuidar de su cobayo cuando vaya de
vacaciones?  Empecé a trabajar con los animales hace doce años y
soy responsable y trabajadora.  Yo sé que las mascotas son miembros
de la familia, así que cuidaré su cobayo como si fuera el mío.  Si
quiere más información, llámeme o envíeme un correo electrónico.

# Technology

**Q1**  Translate these sentences into **English**. Before you start, write down the tense or tenses used in each sentence. The first one has been done for you.

**a)**  Mandaré un mensaje de texto a Ángel. ⟹ ..............**future**..............

**b)**  Podemos buscar una foto en Internet. ⟹ ..................................

**c)**  Flora hacía sus deberes en su portátil. ⟹ ..................................

**d)**  ¿Estás seguro de que has guardado tu trabajo? ⟹ ..................................

**Q2**  Translate the following sentences into **Spanish**. Before you start, underline the possessive adjectives. The first one has been done for you.

**a)**  Do you like <u>my</u> new mobile phone, Julia?

**b)**  Your brother wants a computer for his birthday.

**c)**  Her friend receives lots of spam emails.

**d)**  Our teacher says technology is a great educational tool.

> Possessive adjectives are words like 'my' and 'their'.

**Q3**  Translate these sentences into **English**. Before you start, think about how you will translate the infinitive verbs.

**a)**  Nunca se debe dejar acceso a sus archivos personales a otros.

**b)**  Es importante escoger una contraseña segura.

**c)**  Usaba Internet para acceder a mi cuenta bancaria.

**d)**  Hoy en día, hay que proteger tu identidad en línea.

**e)**  Paula siempre borra sus mensajes después de <u>leerlos</u>.

"Yes, I've tried turning it off and on again."

> Verbs in the infinitive don't always translate into the infinitive in English.

**Q4**  Traduce el texto siguiente al **inglés**.

> En el pasado, la gente usaba cartas y llamadas telefónicas para comunicarse. Hoy en día prefiere usar la tecnología para enviar correos electrónicos o mensajes de texto. Creo que habrá aún más tecnología en el futuro. Si tuviera que <u>dejar</u> de <u>usar</u> mis aparatos*, ¡no sé qué haría!

*el aparato = gadget

When you've finished, check:

☐ Verbs — have you used the right 'person' of the verb?

☐ Flow — does your translation sound natural in English?

Think carefully about translating these verbs — see Q3 for a reminder.

# Social Media

**Q1** Translate these sentences into **English**. Before you start, circle all the radical-changing verbs. The first one has been done for you.

Radical-changing verbs are also known as stem-changing verbs.

a) Todos los días, mi hermano (cuelga) fotos de sí mismo en su blog.

b) Nuestro padre siempre pierde su contraseña.

c) Suelo chatear con mis compañeros de clase en las redes sociales.

d) Por la noche, me acuesto tarde porque navego por la red.

e) Mi madre quiere aprender a utilizar los medios sociales.

**Q2** Translate the adverbs in bold into **Spanish**. Then translate the whole sentence. The first one has been done for you.

a) **Sometimes** I use chat rooms to talk to my cousins in Australia.

.......... **A veces** ..........

b) **Yesterday**, Elena decided to deactivate her account.

..............................

c) When my friend has a problem, she **often** asks for advice on social media.

..............................

d) **Generally**, I don't use chat rooms because they can be dangerous.

..............................

**Q3** Translate these comments about social media into **English**.

a) <u>Lo bueno</u> de las redes sociales es que puedes contactar con tus amigos a cualquier hora.

If 'lo malo' means 'the bad thing', what does 'lo bueno' mean?

b) Es posible ser adicto a los medios sociales. Una amiga mía tenía problemas con sus estudios a causa de su adicción.

**Q4** Translate this passage into **Spanish**.

One disadvantage of social media is that you can be a victim of cyber bullying*. I had to block** people who wrote nasty things about what I had posted. It still worries me, so I don't use social media often. I think it's very important to be safe online.

When you've finished, check:

- [ ] Conjunctions — have you used all the right conjunctions?
- [ ] Vocab — have you translated all the topic vocab correctly?

*cyber bullying = el acoso cibernético

**to block (someone) = bloquear (a alguien)

# Music

**Q1** Translate these sentences into **English**. Before you start, fill in the gaps with the preterite tense of the Spanish verb in brackets. The first one has been done for you.

a) La semana pasada, yo .......**toqué**....... la guitarra con mi padrastro. **(tocar)**

b) Víctor y Gorka ........................ música rock por la mañana. **(escuchar)**

c) Catarina ........................ la letra de sus canciones preferidas. **(aprender)**

d) Mi hermana ........................ a un concierto con su novia. **(ir)**

**Q2** Translate these sentences about music into **Spanish**. Before you start, think carefully about who is doing the action each time (the subject of the verb).

a) Last month, I went to a concert with my aunt and uncle.

b) He downloads music instead of buying CDs.

c) Their music teacher plays the drums in a band.

The llamas weren't impressed by Diego's "musical talents"...

**Q3** The passage below has been translated from Spanish into **English**. Fill in the gaps to complete the translation.

> Estaba escuchando la radio mientras conducía cuando escuché esa canción por primera vez. No sabía nada del grupo pero me enamoré de su música. Compré su álbum y ¡no puedo dejar de escucharlo!

I was ........................................................ while driving when I heard

........................................ for the first time. I didn't know anything about the band

but ........................................................ . I bought their album and

........................................................ !

**Q4** Traduce el texto siguiente al **español**.

You don't use 'jugar' for instruments.

> When I was younger, I used to <u>play</u> the flute. I was a member of an orchestra for three years. Recently, I decided to learn to play a different instrument. I've been playing the piano for six months and I love it. I would like to write my own songs in the future.

When you've finished, check:

☐ Time phrases — do you know how to translate these into Spanish?

☐ Tenses — have you used the correct tenses?

# Cinema and TV

**Q1** Fill in the correct endings for the adjectives, then translate the whole sentence into **English**. The first one has been done for you.

a) La película que vimos tuvo una trama fantástic..**a**.. .

b) Los actores principal...... ganaron un premio por sus papeles.

*Remember — not all adjectives end in 'o' or 'a'.*

c) Odio las series policíac...... porque hay demasiada violencia.

d) Mi programa preferid...... se trata de un chico que se llama Félix.

**Q2** Translate these conversations into **Spanish**. Think carefully about how to translate the verbs — some of them are formed with indirect object pronouns.

a) **Jimena:** I really like cartoons because they make me laugh.

   **Lucas:** Me too, but the news is more important to me. I'm interested in knowing about what's happening in the world.

*Verbs like 'me gusta' use an 'indirect object pronoun + verb' structure.*

b) **Thiago:** Is it true that soap operas annoy you, Maite?

   **Maite:** Yes, I don't like them at all. I don't understand why you watch <u>them</u>, Thiago.

*What is this referring to?*

**Q3** Translate the phrases in bold into **Spanish**, then translate the whole sentence. The first one has been done for you.

a) **On Friday**, I watched TV for more than three hours. ......**El viernes**......

b) We used to go to the cinema **on Sundays** because it was cheaper. ...........................

c) Alejandro is going to see a science fiction film **on Wednesday**. ...........................

d) I watch my favourite programme **on Tuesdays**. ...........................

**Q4** Translate this passage into **English**.

Suelo ver la televisión con mi madre y mi hermana por la tarde. Nos gustan programas distintos, entonces no siempre estamos de acuerdo sobre lo que ver. Mi hermana odiaba los reality shows pero ahora <u>le gustan</u> mucho. Mi madre prefiere ver los concursos* porque le encanta contestar a todas las preguntas.

*un concurso = quiz show

Before you start, check:

☐ Conjunctions — do you know how to translate the conjunctions correctly?

☐ Word order — think about how you will make it sound natural in English.

Look back at Q2 for a reminder on how to translate this.

Section 3 — Technology, Free Time and Customs & Festivals

# Hobbies and Role Models

**Q1** Translate these sentences into **Spanish**. Include subject pronouns to emphasise who is doing each action.

*Subject pronouns are words like 'él' and 'usted'.*

a) They went hiking in Scotland, but we went scuba diving in Portugal.

b) I usually read spy stories, but she prefers to read fantasy stories.

c) You play chess in your free time, but he plays <u>petanque</u>. ← This is a French game, like bowls. It's called 'la petanca' in Spain.

**Q2** Translate these sentences into **English**. Before you start, underline all the demonstrative adjectives. The first one has been done for you.

*Demonstrative adjectives are words like 'this' and 'those'.*

a) Ya he leído <u>ese</u> tebeo, así que voy a comprar otro.

b) Yo quisiera montar a caballo en aquellas montañas.

c) El nuevo libro de este autor sale pronto.

d) Esa atleta es un modelo de conducta para los niños.

The bap — every northerner's roll model.

**Q3** Translate this passage into **English**.
Before you start, answer the questions below.

Think carefully about who is doing the action here.

> Me gustaría ser atleta. Hay muchas personas que me inspiran, sobre todo los atletas que compiten en los Juegos Olímpicos. <u>Los admiro</u> porque entrenan durante cuatro años para representar a su país. Deberían estar orgullosos* de lo que consiguen**.

*orgulloso = proud        **conseguir = to achieve

a) Which two tenses are used in the passage? .................................................................

b) Which English verb does 'compiten' look like? ...........................................................

c) How will you translate 'durante'? .............................................................

**Q4** Translate this passage into **Spanish**.        Will you need to use 'por' or 'para' here?

> My stepsister has written five books <u>for</u> children. She used to write short stories when I was little. I admire her because she's very imaginative and creative. <u>When I'm older</u>, I'd like to be a writer too. However, I'd prefer to write adventure stories or mystery novels for adults.

You'll need to use the subjunctive here.

When you've finished, check:

☐ Pronouns — have you got the order right in Spanish?

☐ Adjective agreement — do all the adjectives agree with the nouns?

 ☐   ☐   ☐  **Section 3 — Technology, Free Time and Customs & Festivals**

# Food

**Q1**  Translate these sentences into **Spanish**.  Before you start, think about how to translate the <u>underlined</u> quantifiers.

a)  He tried <u>many</u> of the dishes on the table.

b)  There are <u>few</u> fruits tastier than peaches.

c)  His parents don't think I eat <u>enough</u> vegetables.

d)  Those are <u>some</u> of the saltiest sausages that I have ever tasted.

What did one vegetable say to another?
Lettuce be friends.

**Q2**  Translate these sentences into **English**.  Before you start, underline all the conjunctions.  The first one has been done for you.

a)  Mi novio salió para comprar bebidas <u>mientras</u> yo preparaba la comida.

b)  Estaba todo listo cuando llegaron nuestros amigos para la fiesta.

c)  Mi hermano no sabe cocinar así que come mucha comida rápida.

d)  Voy a clases de cocina porque quiero aprender a preparar comida rica.

**Q3**  Translate the imperatives in bold using the 'tú' form of the verb.  Then translate the sentences into **Spanish**.  The first one has been done for you.

> Remember that positive and negative imperatives have different endings.

a)  **Add** the sugar to the cream. ⟹ ............... *añade* ...............

b)  Do not **boil** the cabbage. ⟹ ............................................

⟵ Think about the verb that 'hervido' comes from to help you translate this.

c)  After cooking the meat, **chop** the potatoes. ⟹ ..........................................

d)  **Cook** the rice before preparing the sauce. ⟹ .........................................

**Q4**  Traduce el texto siguiente al **inglés**.

Think of 'el efecto invernadero' to help you translate this.

> Mi vecino es vegetariano.  Siempre aprovecha las frutas y verduras que cultiva en su <u>invernadero</u>.  La semana pasada, me invitó a almorzar.  Cocinó un plato de pimientos, zanahorias y guisantes con una <u>salsa</u> picante.  Me gustó tanto que le pedí la receta*.  ¡Espero que yo pueda prepararla tan bien como él!

*la receta = recipe        Look back at Q3 for help translating this.

When you've finished, check:

☐ Pronouns — have you translated all the pronouns correctly?

☐ Flow — does your translation sound natural in English?

# Eating Out

**Q1**   Complete the questions below with the present tense 'usted' form of the verb in brackets. The first one has been done for you.  Then translate the sentences into **English**.

  **a)**  ¿Qué bebida ......**recomienda**...... usted?  Tengo mucha sed.          **(recomendar)**

  **b)**  ¿Qué tipo de comida ........................ cuando tiene hambre?          **(preferir)**

  **c)**  ¿Nos ........................ dar un descuento?          **(poder)**

  **d)**  ¿Nos ........................ la cuenta, por favor?  ¿Está incluida la propina?          **(traer)**

**Q2**   Use 'ser' or 'estar' to translate the words in bold, then translate the sentences into **Spanish**.

  **a)**  My favourite restaurant **is** in the town centre.  ▷ ......**está**......

  **b)**  The pork chops with cream sauce **are** delicious.  ▷ ........................

  **c)**  The waiters **are** very friendly today.  ▷ ........................

  **d)**  The chef **is** preparing our meal.  ▷ ........................

  **e)**  My favourite dessert **is** the apple tart.  ▷ ........................

**Q3**   Agustín and Bianca are having dinner in a restaurant.  Translate their dialogue into **Spanish**. Before you start, think about how you will translate the adverbs of time in bold.

  **a)**  **Agustín:**  Do you **still** want to share a starter*, Bianca?          The verb 'apetecer' means
      **Bianca:**  Yes, <u>I feel like</u> ordering the prawns **again**.          'to feel like'.  You use it in
                                                                the same way as 'gustar'.

  **b)**  **Agustín:**  We should order our drinks **straightaway**.
      **Bianca:**  Good idea, I'd like to try the white wine.

  **c)**  **Agustín:**  I'm really hungry.  I hope our food arrives **soon**.
      **Bianca:**  Me too.  I'm going to have a dessert **afterwards**.
      *starter = un primer plato

**Q4**   Translate this passage into **English**.          How should you translate 'al' + infinitive
                                                          constructions into English?

> ¿Te dije lo que pasó en el restaurante ayer?  El camarero olvidó lo que yo había pedido y me trajo unas chuletas de cerdo en vez de los calamares.  <u>Al llegar</u> a la mesa, la comida estaba fría, así que me quejé al jefe.  Cuando hablé con él, era muy maleducado y no me dio un descuento.  Entonces, no le di propina.

# Sport

**Q1** Translate these sentences into **English**. Before you start, circle the adverbs of frequency. Some of them are more than one word.

*Adverbs of frequency are words like 'often' and 'never'.*

 a) Voy en bici al colegio a diario porque es más rápido que coger el autobús.

 b) Andrea hace patinaje pocas veces porque siempre está ocupada.

 c) Hacemos alpinismo de vez en cuando, cuando <u>el tiempo</u> nos permite.

*This word has two meanings — which do you think is most sensible here?*

 d) Normalmente van al campo de deportes los domingos por la mañana.

**Q2** Translate the comparatives and superlatives in bold into **Spanish**. Then translate the full sentences. The first one has been done for you.

 a) I usually go canoeing with my **younger** sister. ➡ ................ **menor** ........................

 b) Playing football is **better** when the weather is good. ➡ ...........................................

 c) Horse riding is **the worst** sport when it rains. ➡ ..........................................

 d) My brother is **the best** swimmer* in our family. ➡ ...........................................
 *a swimmer = un nadador

**Q3** The passage below has been translated from Spanish into **English**. Fill in the gaps to complete the translation.

> Opino que es muy importante hacer deporte por lo menos dos veces a la semana. Los lunes voy a la pista de atletismo y hago piragüismo los fines de semana. Si hubiera una pista de hielo cerca de mi casa, iría allí para patinar.

I think it's very important to do sport at least ................................................ . On Mondays

I go to .............................................. and I go ........................ at weekends. If there was

an ...................... near my house, I'd ................................................................... .

**Q4** Translate the sentences into **Spanish**. Before you start, underline all the verbs that will use the imperfect tense. The first one has been done for you.

 a) I used to <u>play</u> football when I was younger, but now I play tennis.

 b) Veronica used to love playing hockey and going fishing.

 c) When I arrived at the sports centre, they were playing basketball.

 d) We were near the stadium when we lost the ball.

Section 3 — Technology, Free Time and Customs & Festivals

**Q5**  Fill in the gaps with the correct articles and prepositions. Then translate the sentences into **English**. The first one has been done for you.

a)  Adoro la natación. Voy ....**a la**.... piscina con mis amigos casi todos los días.

b)  Miguel era fanático ........... ciclismo pero ahora prefiere el bádminton.

c)  A menudo vamos ........... colegio los sábados para jugar al netball.

d)  Fuimos ........... parque este fin de semana ........... monopatín.

*You need the preposition 'on' here.*

**Q6**  Translate these comments about sport into **Spanish**.

a)  **Chami:**  I like playing tennis with my friends in the summer.

b)  **Raúl:**  Doing sports is a good way for us to spend time together and have fun.

c)  **Sami:**  I always watch the Winter Olympics because my favourite sport is skiing.

d)  **Clara:**  In the future, I would love to go and see a football match in person.

e)  **Juan:**  I have been horse riding <u>for seven years</u>.  *This is translated literally as 'since it makes seven years'.*

**Q7**  Translate this passage into **Spanish**.  *You'll need to use the verb 'practicar' here.*

My grandad is very sporty.  He <u>goes</u> sailing most days and often plays volleyball* on the beach.  When he was younger, <u>he used to do</u> a lot of adventure sports, but he had to stop because he broke his leg.  He's trying to teach me to sail, but I think it's too difficult.

*volleyball = el voleibol

*Peter hadn't quite got the hang of standing on his skates.*

*Look back to Q4 for a reminder of the imperfect tense.*

**Q8**  Translate this passage into **English**.

*Take a look back at Q2 to help you with this.*

Siempre me ha encantado el rugby.  En mi opinión, es <u>el mejor</u> deporte del mundo.  Tengo muchas ganas de ir a ver un partido.  La próxima semana tendrá lugar un torneo de rugby en el estadio.  Tengo mucha suerte porque mis padres compraron unas entradas para que pudiéramos verlo.

When you've finished, check:

☐  Set phrases — have you translated the set phrases with 'tener' correctly?

☐  Word order — some of the sentences need to be rearranged to make sense in English.

 ☐   ☐   ☐  Section 3 — Technology, Free Time and Customs & Festivals

# Customs and Festivals

**Q1** Translate these sentences into **Spanish**. Before you start, <u>underline</u> the possessive adjectives. The first one has been done for you.

**a)** <u>Your</u> sister loves the fair.

**b)** Their parents danced at the party.

**c)** Christmas is a public holiday in my country.

**d)** Festivals during Easter are our tradition.

**Q2** Think carefully about how you will translate the dates in bold into **Spanish**. Then translate each sentence.

You don't need to translate the underlined name.

Amalia had been sitting for so long, she'd forgotten what day it was...

**a)** <u>Las Fallas</u> is a Valencian festival which starts on **the 15th of March**.

**b)** On **the 6th of January**, many Spaniards celebrate Epiphany.

**c)** All Souls' Day celebrations start at 12am on **the 1st of November**.

**Q3** Translate these comments about bullfighting into **English**. Before you start, think about how you will translate the relative pronouns in bold.

**a)** Este año mis padres van a Pamplona donde hay una fiesta **en la que** la gente corre por las calles seguida por toros.

**b)** Odio las corridas de toros porque son muy crueles. Mi hermano opina **que** son una forma de arte, **lo que** me enfada mucho.

**c)** Un amigo mío tiene un tío **que** era torero. La tauromaquia* es una tradición **de la cual** está muy orgulloso.
   *la tauromaquia = bullfighting

To help translate these relative pronouns, think about which part of the sentence they refer back to.

**Q4** The passage below has been translated from English into **Spanish**. Fill in the gaps to complete the translation.

Don't forget that this is reflexive in Spanish.

> On the 20th of January every year, the citizens of San Sebastián, a city in the north of Spain, celebrate La Tamborrada. Everyone <u>dresses up</u> as chefs or soldiers, then they gather in the main square. The festival starts at midnight and everyone plays the drums for 24 hours without stopping.

.............................................................. cada año los ciudadanos de San

Sebastián, una ciudad en el norte de España, ..................................... La Tamborrada.

Todo el mundo ..................................... cocineros o soldados, luego se reúne en la

plaza mayor. ..................................... a medianoche y todo el mundo

toca los tambores ..................................................................... .

**Q5** Translate these questions into **Spanish**. Remember to think about accents and punctuation.

**a)** Where did you go last Christmas?

**c)** What do you do on Christmas Eve?

**b)** How do you celebrate Epiphany?

**d)** When is Easter this year?


**Q6** Translate this passage into **English**.
Before you start, answer the questions below.

*You don't need to translate Castells.*

> Castells es una de las tradiciones culturales más importantes en
> Cataluña. La gente se reúne en las calles y construye torres humanas
> poniéndose de pie uno encima de otro. Es increíble verlas pero
> puede ser muy peligroso para la gente que participa construyéndolas.

**a)** How will you translate 'torres humanas'? .................................................................

**b)** What does 'encima de' mean? .................................................................

**c)** What is the best way to translate 'construyéndolas'? .................................................


**Q7** Translate these sentences into **Spanish**. Before you start, circle all the verbs and think about whether each one is regular or irregular. The first one has been done for you.

**a)** My cousin (went) to Columbia to celebrate the Carnaval de Barranquilla.
She saw the Gran Parada and took part in the Batalla de Flores.

*You don't need to translate the underlined words.*

**b)** Next year, my mother and I will travel to Buñol. We will visit
my uncles who participate in La Tomatina every year.

**c)** If you go to Bilbao in August, it's worth seeing the Aste Nagusia
celebrations. Watch the parades*, try the food and enjoy the day. ← You'll need to use the imperative to translate this sentence.
*parade = un desfile


**Q8** Traduce el texto siguiente al **inglés**.

This comes from the verb 'luchar'.

> Este verano fui a Jávea. Participé en una fiesta que recuerda la lucha entre
> dos culturas diferentes para gobernar la tierra*. Había muchos desfiles
> coloridos, conciertos de música y fuegos artificiales**. Aprendí mucho
> sobre la historia de la zona y me gustaría volver a celebrarla en el futuro.

*gobernar la tierra = to rule the land    **los fuegos artificiales = fireworks

When you've finished, check:

☐ Flow — are you happy that the passage sounds natural in English?

☐ Tenses — have you translated each tense correctly?

☺ ☐   ☺ ☐   ☺ ☐   **Section 3 — Technology, Free Time and Customs & Festivals**

# Mixed Practice

**Q1**   Translate the following statements into **Spanish**.

**a)**   Bruno often uses social networks to share his band's music.

**b)**   It was cheaper to buy the concert tickets online.

**c)**   I've seen lots of adverts on social media for a new comedy.

**d)**   She wanted to watch the TV show on the Internet, but it's not available anymore.

**Q2**   Translate these sentences into **English**.    *Use the context and your knowledge of the individual words to help you work this out.*

**a)**   A Hernando le regalaron <u>un lector de libros electrónicos</u> para su cumpleaños pero no lo utiliza.  Siempre ha preferido los libros de papel.

**b)**   A Renata le encanta leer.  Nunca la veo sin un periódico en la mano. Sus padres preferirían que hiciera más deporte pero a ella no le gusta.

**c)**   Tengo muchas aficiones.  Los miércoles suelo practicar artes marciales. Los fines de semana me gusta jugar a juegos de mesa* con mis compañeros.
*los juegos de mesa = board games

**Q3**   Translate these sentences about music into **Spanish**.

*How do you translate the reflexive pronoun 'himself' into Spanish?*

**a)**   Álvaro records <u>himself</u> when he plays the trumpet and puts the videos on the internet.

**b)**   Playing the clarinet used to be one of their favourite pastimes.

**c)**   We watched a documentary about the use of castanets in traditional Spanish music.

**d)**   My mum loves opera music.  She often listens to it on her laptop.

**e)**   I follow my favourite musician on social media in order to listen to her new songs.
*musician = un/a músico/a

**Q4**   Traduce el texto siguiente al **español**.

My mum thinks I'm lazy because I'm always surfing the Internet.  When I was little, I used to play basketball outside with my friends.  Now I prefer to stay at home and play video games.  We often have arguments about how much time I spend in front of the computer.

Rochelle was hoping no-one would notice that she'd glued the ball to her hand.

Section 3 — Technology, Free Time and Customs & Festivals

# Mixed Practice

**Q5**  Translate this passage into **English**.

> El año pasado mi amiga y yo visitamos un pueblo aislado donde hay una
> fiesta que celebra la cosecha* de las uvas.  Es un evento muy famoso así que
> había muchas cámaras de televisión que estaban grabando toda la acción.
> Nos entrevistaron unos periodistas y ¡nos vimos en las noticias ese mismo día!

*la cosecha = harvest

**Q6**  Traduce la conversación siguiente al **español**.

**Gael:**  Are you coming to the cinema?  We're going to see the new science fiction film.

**Isaías:**  I said that I'd prepare dinner for my family tonight.  What time are you going to go?

**Gael:**  We're meeting outside the cinema at 7 o'clock,
but the film doesn't start until half past 7.

**Isaías:**  I'll send you a text if I can come, but I doubt that I can.

**Q7**  Traduce las frases siguientes al **inglés**.

**a)**  Nerea decidió ir a la fiesta después de ver las fotos de las
procesiones que su amigo había colgado en las redes sociales.

**b)**  Mis videojuegos preferidos son esos en los cuales se puede
hacer deporte.  Tengo unos que usan la realidad virtual.

**c)**  Cocinar es su pasión desde hace once años.  Siempre él busca nuevas recetas
por el Internet.  Cuando sea mayor él quiere tener su propia pastelería.

**Q8**  Jerónimo has written this film review for his school newspaper.  Translate it into **English**.

> **Los Guantes del Diablo***  ☆ ☆ ☆ ☆ ☆
>
> Vi esta película de terror fenomenal el jueves.  <u>Se basa</u> en un programa
> de televisión muy popular del mismo nombre.  Tiene mucha acción y una
> banda sonora emocionante.  Se trata de un hombre que encuentra unos
> guantes creados por el diablo.  La recomendaría a todos mis amigos.

Which English
verb does this
Spanish verb
look like?

*el diablo = the devil

# Mixed Practice

**Q9** Translate these comments about watching sport into **English**.

**a)** Prefiero ver los torneos de rugby en persona que en la tele. Hay un ambiente mejor en el estadio que en mi salón.

**b)** Ver deporte en línea ha llegado a ser muy popular porque es muy conveniente. Se puede ver partidos y torneos sin salir de la casa.

**c)** Como futbolista, quiero que los aficionados vengan al estadio a ver los partidos. Es mucho más emocionante que verlos en sus ordenadores.

**Q10** Translate this advert for a café into **Spanish**.

> You don't need to translate the name of the café.

Stitchton Café is the perfect place to relax after playing sport on the beach. Our balconies offer great views of the volleyball courts. Every Saturday in June, there will be music and dancing from 8pm. To <u>kick things off</u>, after the volleyball tournament this week, we're having a beach party.

*balcony = un balcón

Translate this as 'to start' or 'to begin'.

**Q11** Iker and Nina are talking about a food festival in their town. Translate their conversation into **English**.

**a)** **Iker:** ¿Fuiste a la festival de comida el sábado? Había tantísimos platos y me encantaron todos.

**b)** **Nina:** ¡Claro! Fui con mis padres. Probamos unos filetes de ternera cocinados con ajo y pimienta.

**c)** **Iker:** ¡Qué rico! ¿Visteis el concurso por la tarde?

Pay close attention to the tenses used in the last sentence.

**d)** **Nina:** No lo vimos. ¿Cuál ganó? Si tuviera que elegir mi plato preferido, sería la paella de pollo y gambas.

**Q12** Translate this passage into **Spanish**.

Fabiana's idol* has just opened a new restaurant in the town centre. She has watched his cookery programmes on TV since she was very small, so she'd love to try his dishes. The only problem is, she hasn't been able to reserve a table yet because the restaurant is very popular.

*an idol = un ídolo

# Where You Live

**Q1** Complete the Spanish sentences with the correct imperfect tense form of the verb in brackets. The first one has been done for you. Then translate the sentences into **English**.

a) Cuando era pequeño, él ........_vivía_........ en el campo.          **(vivir)**

*Remember to check your accents in the imperfect tense.*

b) Los chicos ........................ al colegio.          **(ir)**

c) Yo ........................ que andar al supermercado.          **(tener)**

d) Nosotros ........................ el mercado de flores.          **(visitar)**

**Q2** Tick the sentences where the underlined nouns are feminine in **Spanish**, then translate the sentences.

a) The <u>city</u> has quite a small population.          ☐

b) The <u>town hall</u> is in the pedestrian zone.          ☐

c) There is a beautiful <u>mosque</u> in the town centre.          ☐

d) I like to go to the <u>pastry shop</u> in our village.          ☐

*Thiago had just found out how close his house was to the cake shop.*

**Q3** Read the following text, answer the questions below and then translate the passage into **English**.

Carmen acaba de mudarse a Santiago de Compostela, una ciudad en el noroeste de España. A ella le gusta la ciudad porque es muy animada y tiene una iglesia magnífica. El año pasado, vivió en Barcelona porque siempre había querido vivir cerca del mar.

a) What does 'acaba de mudarse' mean in English? ..............................................

b) How will you translate 'noroeste'? ..............................................

c) Which tense is 'había querido' written in? ..............................................

**Q4** Traduce el texto siguiente al **español**.

*You'll need the verb 'hacer' to translate this.*

I like living in a city because it's fun and there's always something to do. <u>Two years ago,</u> a big restaurant and a modern nightclub opened their doors near the harbour. I wouldn't like to live in the countryside because there aren't many shops and it's boring <u>there</u>.

Before you start, check:

☐ Tenses — do you know which tenses you need for each sentence?

☐ Adjectives — will their position in the sentence need to change in English?

— Which adverb should you use for this?

☺ ☐   ☺ ☐   ☺ ☐

# The Home

**Q1**  Read the following passage then fill in the gaps in the **English** translation.

> Vivo en una pensión en las afueras de la ciudad. A mí no me gusta
> porque me siento aislado. Antes, vivía en un piso en el centro de
> la ciudad pero perdí mi empleo y tuve que mudarme de casa.

I live in a ............................................ on the ........................ of town. I don't like it

because ............................................ . Before this, I lived in a ........................ in the

............................................ but I lost my job and had to ............................................ .

**Q2**  Complete the Spanish sentences with the correct present tense form of 'ser' or 'estar'. The first one has been done for you. Then translate the sentences into **English**.

**a)**  La casa de mi familia ........**es**........ pequeñita.

**b)**  El salón ........................ enfrente de la cocina.

**c)**  Ambos cuartos de baño ........................ en la segunda planta.

**d)**  Las escaleras en nuestra casa ........................ <u>estrechas</u>. ◄ This has a similar meaning to 'delgado'.

**Q3**  Translate the phrases in bold containing prepositions. The first one has been done for you. Then translate the sentences into **Spanish**.

**a)**  The picture is hanging **on the wall**. ⇨ ........**en la pared**........

**b)**  There is a small river **next to their house**. ⇨ ............................................

**c)**  The farm is situated **in the mountains**. ⇨ ............................................

**d)**  They are moving **into a new flat**. ⇨ ............................................

**Q4**  Traduce el siguiente texto al **español**.

— Think about the Spanish word for 'birthday'.

> I moved out of home when <u>I turned</u> eighteen years old. I didn't like
> sharing a room with my sister. In my flat, my favourite room is the kitchen
> because it is big and there are comfortable chairs at the dining table.
> Unfortunately, my bedroom is <u>very small</u> and doesn't have a window.

— Have a look at Q2 to help you translate this.

# Home Life

**Q1** <u>Underline</u> all the adverbs in these sentences. The first one has been done for you. Then translate the sentences into **English**.

a) <u>Cada día</u>, me despierto temprano para sacar a pasear al perro.

b) De vez en cuando, desayuno cereales con poca leche.

c) Todos los días, me ducho antes de acostarme y nunca me olvido.

d) Almuerzo en el instituto a menudo y casi nunca salgo a comer.

"I told you the hairbrush makes my fur frizzy Jessica... now look at me."

**Q2** Translate the verbs in bold into **Spanish**. You'll need a reflexive verb for each one. Then translate the whole sentence.

a) I **get up** early but I am always tired. ⟶ ........**me levanto**........

b) Robert **wakes up** late at the weekends. ⟶ ................................

c) Laura always **sits down** when she gets home. ⟶ ................................

d) My parents **get dressed** while they listen to the radio. ⟶ ................................

**Q3** Samara and Carlos are talking about their morning routines. Translate their conversation into **Spanish**. Use the 'tú' form because they know each other.

a) **Samara:** My mum always <u>wakes me up</u> at 7am for breakfast. ⟵ Be careful with pronoun order.
**Carlos:** I get up at 6.30am to shower before <u>having breakfast</u>. ⟵ Use the infinitive here, not the '–ing' form of the verb.

b) **Samara:** Do you make your bed before or after you shower?
**Carlos:** I often forget to do it because I'm not very organised in the morning.

c) **Samara:** I usually do my chores* after school. Yesterday I mowed the lawn.
**Carlos:** I had to take the rubbish out last night. It was disgusting!
*chores = las tareas domésticas

**Q4** Adrián's dad is talking about his morning routine. Translate the text into **English**.

Creo que levantarse temprano es la mejor manera de empezar el día. Se puede hacer ejercicio, pasear al perro, ducharse y preparar el desayuno para todos antes de que se despierten. Los niños nunca se acuestan cuando <u>les pido</u> así que es difícil levantarlos por la mañana.

Think about how the word order will change in English.

When you've finished, check:
☐ Verbs — have you used the right 'person'?
☐ Infinitives — have you translated them all correctly?

**Section 4 — Where You Live**

# Shopping

**Q1**  Fill in the correct endings for the adjectives, then translate the sentences into **English**.  The first one has been done for you.

a)  Busco una camisa de algodón blanc **a** .

b)  Quisiera comprar unos pantalones negr..... .

c)  Quiero una bufanda roj..... para llevar con mi abrigo amarill..... .

d)  Me gustaría comprar unos pendientes azul..... .

Shopping 101:
Always check for holes before
you leave the shop...

**Q2**  Translate the demonstrative adjectives in bold into **Spanish**, then translate the whole sentence.  The first has been done for you.

a)  I would like one hundred grams of **this** cheese.  ▷  ..........**este**..........

b)  I need a dozen of **those** eggs, please.  ▷  ....................

c)  I'd like a packet of **these** grapes and half of **that** ham.  ▷  ...............................

d)  Give me half a kilo of **those** carrots over there.  ▷  ....................  ◀— Look at the whole sentence for a clue on which word to use here.

**Q3**  Fill in the gaps with the correct indefinite article (un, una, unos, unas).  The first one has been done for you.  Then translate the sentences into **English**.

a)  Él quiere ...**un**.... bote de mermelada y ........... caja de galletas de chocolate.

b)  Me hace falta .......... kilo de cebollas y .......... latas de tomate.

c)  Ella necesita .......... botellas de aceite de oliva y .......... barra de pan.

d)  Deme .......... pedazo de esta tarta de frutas y .......... trozos de ese pastel.

**Q4**  Translate these sentences into **Spanish**.  Before you start, think about how you will translate the underlined phrases below, which contain quantifiers.

a)  This shop only has <u>a few</u> different sizes.  ◀— Use 'la talla' to talk about the size of clothes in Spanish.

b)  Do you have <u>enough money</u> to buy all these clothes?

c)  There were <u>so many people</u> in the department store on Saturday.

Make sure the quantifier agrees with the noun.

d)  I go to the same shop to buy my clothes because it has <u>lots of styles</u>.

e)  I bought <u>too many dresses</u> in the sales and I need to return them.

**Q5** Translate the bold sections into **Spanish** using the immediate future tense (formed with 'ir'). The first one has been done for you. Then translate each sentence.

a) **I'm going to return** this skirt tomorrow. ⟹ ............**Voy a devolver**............

b) My sister **is going to ask** the cashier for a refund. ⟹ ......................................

c) I think **they're going to complain** to the manager. ⟹ ......................................

d) **We're going to exchange** <u>these</u> dresses for <u>those</u>. ⟹ ......................................

**Q6** Translate the following sentences into **English**.

a) Deme otro cartón de zumo de uvas; uno lleno esta vez.

b) Quiero un bocadillo de queso con lechuga y varios paquetes de patatas fritas.

c) La receta es muy complicada. Nos falta la mitad de lo que necesitamos.

d) En el supermercado, hay que pesar las verduras antes de llevarlas a la caja.

e) Juan y Carla necesitan ir de compras más a menudo porque su nevera siempre está vacía.

f) Tu hermanastra necesitaba comprar todos los ingredientes antes de empezar a cocinar.

**Q7** Traduce el texto siguiente al **inglés**.

> Yo iba al centro para comprar comida pero ahora la hago en línea. Es muy conveniente ya que se puede hacer en cualquier momento del día y no hay que salir de casa. Sin embargo, es fácil gastar dinero sin pensarlo. Todavía prefiero ir a las tiendas para comprar la ropa.

When you've finished, check:

☐ Tenses — have you used the right tenses in each sentence?

☐ Conjunctions — have you translated them correctly?

**Q8** Blanca is returning a tracksuit to a clothes shop. Translate her conversation with the shopkeeper into **Spanish**.

*You'll need to use the 'usted' form because they don't know each other.*

**Blanca:** I would like to exchange this blue tracksuit please.

**David:** Is there a problem?

**Blanca:** The sleeves* are too short. Also, the zip** on the trousers is broken.

**David:** I'll bring you another one. What size do you need?

**Blanca:** Size forty, please.

**David:** <u>Here you go</u>. I have given you a discount. ⟵ This is translated as 'here you have it'.

*sleeves = las mangas    **zip = el cierre

# Directions

**Q1**  Translate these sentences into **Spanish**. Before you start, think about how you will translate the ordinal numbers.

*Don't confuse this with the word for 'four'.*

a)  Take the fifth road after the traffic lights.

b)  It's after the second bridge.

c)  Follow the <u>fourth</u> road to the end.

d)  It is the third building on the left.

**Q2**  Complete the sentences with the correct Spanish translation of the preposition in brackets. The first one has been done for you. Then translate the sentences into **English**.

a)  El aparcamiento está ......**detrás de**...... la biblioteca.  **(behind)**

b)  El polideportivo está allá, ...................... la iglesia.  **(next to)**

c)  La peluquería se encuentra ...................... la carnicería.  **(opposite)**

d)  La librería está situada ...................... el estanco y la panadería.  **(between)**

e)  La comisaría está ...................... ayuntamiento.  **(in front of)**

*You'll need to use a contraction ('de' + masculine article) here.*

**Q3**  Fill in the missing **Spanish** words to complete the translation. Use the imperative in the 'usted' form for each one.

*Use the verb 'doblar' to translate this.*

> Take the first street on the left and then <u>turn</u> right at the end of the road. Go past the traffic lights and continue straight on. At the bridge, turn right and follow the street. Cross the square, and the accommodation will be a few steps away to the left.

......**Tome**...... la primera calle a la izquierda, y después ...................... a la

derecha al final de la calle. ...................... los semáforos y ......................

todo recto. En el puente, ...................... a la derecha y ...................... la

calle. ...................... la plaza y el alojamiento estará a un paso a la izquierda.

**Q4**  Traduce el siguiente texto al **inglés**.

*Look at the rest of the sentence for clues on how to translate this.*

> Para llegar a la granja, es mejor ir en coche <u>ya que</u> está un poco aislada. Pase la estación y doble a la derecha cuando vea el segundo semáforo. Luego, cruce el puente y siga todo recto. Estará a unos quinientos metros de ahí, al final de la calle.

# Weather

**Q1** Use the preterite tense of either 'haber', 'hacer' or 'estar' to complete these sentences correctly. Then translate the sentences into **English**.

a) En el centro de España, ......**hubo**...... mucho viento.

b) ...................... frío en el norte de Inglaterra.

c) En el noroeste de Francia, ...................... caluroso.

d) El viernes, ...................... chubascos en el sur.

Dad was jet-washing the drive so Luna took the chance to try out her new raincoat.

**Q2** Underline the adverbs of place in the sentences below. The first one has been done for you. Then translate the sentences into **Spanish**.

> Adverbs of place are words like 'aquí' and 'ahí'.

a) It's very hot <u>over there</u>.

b) It's cloudy and cold everywhere.

c) It's raining here but it's only windy there.

d) There are thunder and lightning storms nearby.

**Q3** Answer the questions below, then translate the passage into **English**.

> Me encanta cuando hace sol porque se puede ir a la playa. Sería ideal <u>si no estuviera</u> húmedo nunca porque no duermo bien por la noche. Tampoco me siento bien cuando está muy seco. Cuando está tormentoso, me gusta ver los relámpagos.

a) Which tense is underlined in the passage? ................................................

b) How will you translate 'tampoco'? ................................................

c) What are 'los relámpagos'? ................................................

**Q4** Jaime has received a postcard from his friends. Translate it into **Spanish**.

> The temperature here in Great Britain is very different to Spain. The day we visited London, the weather wasn't bad in the morning but it started to rain in the afternoon. We are currently in Wales, where it is windy and cold. We will travel to Scotland tomorrow. <u>I hope it's sunny and warm there</u>!

Think about which tenses you need to use in this sentence.

When you've finished, check:

☐ Verbs — have you chosen the correct verb to talk about weather?

☐ Tenses — have you translated all the different tenses correctly?

 ☐   ☐   ☐

Section 4 — Where You Live

# Mixed Practice

**Q1**    Traduce las conversaciones siguientes al **español**.

    **a)**  **Rosa:**    The forecast for the weekend is good, so I want to buy this dress.

          **María**:   I love the colour but it's too big.  I'll bring you a smaller one.

    **b)**  **Juan:**    Can I borrow your blue jacket tonight?  I don't want to be cold at the party.

          **Diego:**  Of course, it's on the chair next to the door.

    **c)**  **Pilar:**    It's so windy that my umbrella has broken.  Can I buy another here?

          **Sofía:**   Yes and there's a discount if you buy two.

**Q2**    Translate the text below into **English**.

> Guillermo vivía en las montañas.  A él le encantaba jugar
> al rugby allí, pero estaba tormentoso a menudo.  Cuando
> el equipo no podía jugar afuera, iba al polideportivo en las
> afueras de la ciudad.  Ahora, él juega para un equipo en una
> ciudad cercana y espera que el rugby pueda ser su carrera.

Francis had taken his 'star player' award to heart.

**Q3**    Translate these sentences into **Spanish**.   (AQA & EDEXCEL)

    **a)**  My grandparents live in the countryside.  It used to be a quiet place but a local
          company built a factory nearby.  Now there's lots of noise and smoke.

    **b)**  My parents are going to move house when my younger sisters
          go to university because their house will be too big for them.

    **c)**  Unfortunately the heating doesn't work in my new flat, so I will need to call an
          engineer to repair it.  However, I really like the flat because <u>it's light</u> and <u>spacious</u>.

                          Translate this as 'it has light'.

**Q4**    Translate the passage below into **English**.

> Ayer fuimos a la costa porque hacía mucho sol.  Nadamos en el mar y después
> pasamos el resto del día sentados en la playa, hasta que empezó a hacer frío.
> Quería ir de compras esta mañana porque voy a una fiesta la semana que
> viene.  Desafortunadamente, mi madre no pudo llevarme al centro comercial.

# Mixed Practice

**Q5** Traduce las frases siguientes al **español**.

**a)** I don't like my neighbourhood because it's always too busy and the traffic is terrible.

**b)** I'd like to live somewhere else. I'd prefer to live in the countryside where it's quieter.

**c)** This morning I went to the bookshop for my parents and I've just got back.

**d)** My sister does the food shopping and my brother cleans the kitchen.

**e)** I started working at the butcher's last week but I don't know much about meat yet.

**f)** I will learn how to cut and weigh the meat for customers* next week.
*customers = los clientes

**Q6** Marta is talking about her old house. Translate the passage below into **English**.

> En nuestra vieja casa, el salón estaba enfrente de la cocina y había un cuarto de baño pequeño al lado izquierdo de la escalera. En nuestra casa <u>actual</u>, la cocina está al final del pasillo en la primera planta. Cuando redecoremos la casa, tendremos que guardar los muebles en el sótano para que no se dañen.

Watch out for false friends.

**Q7** Laura and Nico are making plans to meet up. Translate their dialogue into **English**.

AQA & EDEXCEL

Think about how you could make this sound natural in English.

**a)** **Laura:** ¿Vienes a almorzar el jueves que viene?
 **Nico:** Sí, <u>lo espero con impaciencia</u>. ¿Vives cerca del puerto, no?

**b)** **Laura:** Sí, pasa el museo que está al lado de la comisaría y sigue esa calle al final.
 **Nico:** ¿Cómo es la casa?

**c)** **Laura:** Es la tercera casa adosada al lado derecho de la calle.
 **Nico:** Perfecto. Te llamaré si no puedo encontrarla.

**Q8** Translate these sentences into **Spanish**.

**a)** The best place to park when it rains is the car park next to the town hall.

**b)** It's going to be icy this weekend. I'm going to get the bus into the town centre instead of driving because it's safer.

**c)** Yesterday's storm damaged several boats in the harbour.

**d)** It used to snow a lot in winter. The factories in town often had to close because the workers couldn't get there.

# Mixed Practice

**Q9**  Juan and Emilia are organising a shopping trip.
Translate their conversation into **Spanish**.

a)  **Juan:**  Do you want to go shopping tomorrow?  I need to return some shoes.
   **Emilia:**  Yes, I'll come with you.  I would like to buy a new swimming costume.

b)  **Juan:**  If it's not raining, let's meet in the park in front of the bus station at 10 o'clock.
   **Emilia:**  Okay, but if the weather's bad, let's go to the café we went to last month.

c)  **Juan:**  I don't remember where that is.  Is it near the police station?
   **Emilia:**  It's at the end of the main street, next to the museum on the left.

**Q10**  Translate the following passage into **English**.

> Cuando voy de compras, me gusta andar al centro en vez de conducir.  Sin
> embargo, volver con bolsas llenas es difícil cuando hace tanto calor como
> hoy.  Mañana tengo que comprar muchas cosas y espero que esté menos
> húmedo que hoy.  No podía ir ayer porque no había cobrado* mi sueldo.

*cobrar = to get paid

**Q11**  Translate the sentences below into **Spanish**.

a)  Last week, I got up at half past six, I walked the dog and I got dressed
for school.  However, school had to close because of the snow.

b)  On Thursday I was washing my car, when I saw my neighbour.
He was leaving the house with his wife to go for a walk.

c)  I'm going to clean my flat later.  Some friends are coming for dinner
on Friday and I won't have time to do it before they arrive.

**Q12**  Traduce el texto siguiente al **inglés**.

> En dos semanas, será el cumpleaños de mi tío.
> Siempre yo le compraba un pastel de la misma
> pastelería.  Sin embargo, se cerró el mes pasado, así
> que tendré que hacerle uno yo mismo.  Creo que me
> harán falta medio kilo de harina, media docena de
> huevos, un paquete de azúcar y algo de mantequilla.

"Did you see that, Linda?
I CROSSED THE ROAD."

# Healthy Living

**Q1**  Complete the sentences with the preterite tense of the verbs in brackets.
The first one has been done for you.  Then translate the sentences into **English**.

a)  Por la mañana, nosotros ........**fuimos**........ juntos a la piscina.  **(ir)**

b)  Ella ...................... mucha agua después de su clase de boxeo.  **(beber)**

c)  La noche pasada, yo ...................... más de nueve horas.  **(dormir)**

d)  Ayer yo ...................... al bádminton con mis amigos.  **(jugar)**

**Q2**  Complete the Spanish sentences with either 'por'
or 'para'.  Then translate the sentences into **English**.

> Think carefully about the function of 'por' and 'para' in each sentence.

a)  Hay que comer bien ..........**para**.......... tener bastante energía.

b)  La gente suele hacer ejercicio ...................... una o dos horas a la vez.

c)  Ella corre ...................... las calles cada sábado al polideportivo.

d)  ...................... mantenerse en forma, los deportistas tienen que seguir una vida saludable.

**Q3**  Translate the passage below into **Spanish**.  Before you start, underline the
verbs which require you to use the infinitive.  Use the formal 'you' form.

> Doing exercise every week will help you to keep fit.  <u>Leading</u>
> a healthy life means you should eat a balanced diet.  Avoiding
> junk food is important and you should try to eat healthily.
> It is also important to drink lots of water and sleep enough.

You'll need the verb 'llevar' here.

Laura was wondering if running from revision counted as cardio.

**Q4**  Traduce el texto siguiente al **inglés**.

Look back at Q3 if you're stuck with this.

> Creo que en general, <u>llevo</u> una vida saludable.
> Intento comer bien y hacer ejercicio a menudo.
> Debería comer más fruta pero no me gusta mucho.
> En su lugar, intento comer muchas verduras.
> Cuando era pequeño, mis padres nunca me daban
> pescado, pero ahora lo como varias veces por semana.

When you've finished, check:

☐ Vocab — are you happy that you've translated the topic vocab correctly?

☐ Flow — does your translation sound natural in English?

# Unhealthy Living

**Q1** Translate these sentences into **Spanish**. Before you start, think carefully about how you will translate the negative phrases. Use a different negative expression in each sentence.

**a)** I don't like the smell of smoke.

**d)** I don't know anyone who drinks alcohol.

**b)** None of my friends take drugs.

**e)** Neither my mum nor my dad has ever smoked.

**c)** I'd never want to harm my lungs.

**f)** My aunt doesn't eat junk food anymore.

**Q2** Translate the infinitive constructions in bold into **English**.
The first one has been done for you. Then translate each sentence.

**a)** Mi tío bebía zumo **en vez de beber** alcohol. ▷▶ .............**instead of drinking**..............

**b)** Debes hacer algo para relajarte **antes de acostarte**. ▷▶ ......................................

**c)** **Después de oler** el humo de cigarillo, me encontré mal. ▷▶ ......................................

**d)** Preferiríamos ir a bailar **en lugar de emborracharnos**. ▷▶ ......................................

**Q3** Translate the dialogues below into **Spanish**.

**a)** **Ruiz:** My dad quit smoking last year. It was very difficult.

**Juan:** My mum still smokes but I want her to <u>stop</u>. ◀ *Use a form of 'dejar' to translate 'stop' here.*

**b)** **Rosa:** When I go outside in the summer, I always wear a hat.

**Gabi:** Me too. It's important to protect yourself from the sun.

**c)** **Samara:** I wouldn't want to take drugs. It is very hard to stop.

**Jaime:** Yes, and people often have bad <u>withdrawal symptoms</u>.

↖ *This is singular in Spanish.*

**Q4** Translate the passage below into **English**. *Think about what 'peor'*
*means to help you with this.*

En mi colegio, hay algunos jóvenes que toman drogas.
El problema se ha <u>empeorado</u> recientemente y podría
ser a causa de la presión de grupo. <u>Yo no quiero nunca</u>
tomar drogas. Los que toman drogas encuentran difícil
concentrarse en sus estudios. Siempre se sienten cansados
y podrían desarollar problemas de salud en el futuro.

*The only smoking area left in town had got a bit crowded.*

*Q1 will help you translate this construction.*

# Illnesses

**Q1**  Complete the following sentences using the present tense of the verb 'doler'. Then translate them into **English**.

*'Doler' works like 'gustar'.*

**a)**  A mi hermana ........................ la garganta.

**c)**  A mí ........................ las rodillas.

**b)**  A nosotros ........................ las piernas.

**d)**  A ella ........................ la cabeza.

**Q2**  Translate the sentences below into **Spanish**. Before you start, underline the phrases that require the future tense. The first one has been done for you.

**a)**  <u>He will have to</u> go to hospital because he has broken his leg.

**b)**  She woke up with earache, so we'll take her to a doctor.

**c)**  The problem of youth obesity won't get better without intervention from the government.

**d)**  If his panic attack doesn't <u>go away</u>, he will need an ambulance.

*Use the verb 'desaparecer' here.*

**e)**  Next year, it will be compulsory to vaccinate* children.

*to vaccinate = vacunar

**Q3**  Translate the following dialogues into **English**.

*Think about how you might translate this.*

**a)**  **Jacob:**  Mi madre quería que yo te preguntara si tienes alergias.

**Mateo:**  Tuve una reacción a las nueces hace dos años pero nunca más <u>desde entonces</u>.

**b)**  **María:**  Cuando respiro, me siento como que no tengo aire suficiente en los pulmones.

**Alexa:**  ¿Tienes asma? Deberías pedir una cita con un médico.

**c)**  **Remi:**  Mi hermano se cayó el lunes y se rompió el brazo.

**Luis:**  ¡Qué pena! Me rompí el brazo el año pasado y tuve que tener cirugía*.

*cirugía = surgery

**Q4**  Translate what David is saying into **Spanish**.

*Look back to Q2 for a reminder on the future tense.*

> A few months ago, I was very ill but I'm feeling better now. I lost a lot of weight and I felt tired all the time. The doctor says that I am stressed*. <u>I will need to</u> take time off work so I can get better. I hope to feel better soon.

*stressed = estresado/a

When you've finished, check:

☐ Verbs — have you used the right 'person' of the verb?

☐ Tenses — think carefully about whether you need to use the subjunctive anywhere.

# Environmental Problems

**Q1**  Translate the following sentences into **Spanish**. Before you start, think about how you will translate the underlined quantifiers.

*Quantifiers go before the noun and often agree with it.*

**a)** People throw away <u>too much</u> rubbish and I don't think it's necessary.

**b)** There are <u>so many</u> simple things we can do to help the environment.

**c)** We don't recycle <u>enough</u> plastic, and this damages the environment.

**d)** <u>Few</u> people realise the severity of the problem of climate change.

**Q2**  Conjugate the verbs in bold in either the future or conditional tense, as indicated. The first one has been done for you. Then translate the new sentences into **English**.

**a)** Nosotros ....**apagaremos**.... nuestros aparatos electrónicos.  **(apagar – future)**

**b)** Yo soñaba que ya no ......................... basura en las playas.  **(ver – conditional)**

**c)** El gobierno ......................... cuando vea el daño.  **(actuar – future)**

**d)** Si tuvieran tiempo, ellos ......................... en vez de conducir.  **(andar – conditional)**

**e)** Vosotros ......................... pronto los efectos de los residuos.  **(saber – future)**

**Q3**  Complete these opinions with the present subjunctive 'we' form of the verb in brackets. The first one has been done for you. Then translate the sentences into **English**.

**a)** Es importante que ....**cuidemos**.... de nuestro planeta.  **(cuidar)**

**b)** Es terrible que no ......................... bastante.  **(reciclar)**

**c)** Es triste que ......................... tantos árboles en la selva amazónica.  **(cortar)**

**d)** Es esencial que ......................... algo para reducir el uso de plástico.  **(hacer)**

**e)** Es crucial que ......................... más energía renovable.  **(usar)**

**Q4**  Translate these sentences which use conjunctions into **Spanish**.

*Conjunctions are words like 'o' and 'así que' that link ideas together.*

**a)** We should turn off the lights so we can save energy.

**b)** Climate change worries me because it is not getting better.

**c)** Plastic can be dangerous for sea creatures if people throw it in the sea.

**d)** Companies should help to <u>develop</u> renewable energy and new ways to use it.

*Think about 'el desarrollo' to help you translate this.*

**Q5** Translate the words in bold into **Spanish**. Each time, think about whether to use the preterite or imperfect tense. Then translate the whole sentence.

a) At first, people **didn't believe** in global warming. ➡ ......**no creía**......

This is translated as 'solar energy'.

b) We **learned** a lot about <u>solar power</u> in our class yesterday. ➡ ......................

c) We **used to know** very little about the ozone layer. ➡ ....................

d) Last week, the government **decided** <u>to lower</u> pollution levels. ➡ ......................

Use the verb 'bajar' to translate this.

**Q6** Matías is talking about pollution in his city. Translate the following passage into **English**.

Creo que el gobierno debe hacer más para reducir la polución. Vivo en Lima y hay tanto tráfico que produce <u>contaminación</u> medioambiental y acústica\*. Es esencial que enseñemos a los niños el daño serio que la contaminación causa.

\*acústica = noise

This means the same as 'polución'.

Ella realised that she was going to need a much brighter high-vis jacket.

**Q7** Traduce las opiniones siguientes al **inglés**.

a) **Pedro:** Hay que combatir el problema de la deforestación.

b) **Raquel:** Tenemos que hacer algo porque desaparece rápidamente la selva.

c) **Luisa:** No creo que la responsabilidad sea solo del gobierno.

d) **Dante:** En mi opinión, el problema más grave es la contaminación de los ríos.

e) **Enzo:** La gente <u>echa la culpa</u> al efecto invernadero por problemas medioambientales.

This is a set phrase — you can't translate it literally.

**Q8** Translate the following passage into **Spanish**. How will you translate this tense?

Natural disasters <u>have always been</u> a problem but they are more frequent now than before. There are floods, hurricanes and droughts in the news every week. Everyone's actions contribute to climate change and the situation is very serious. We must do something to protect the Earth and <u>prevent further</u> damage.

Translate this as 'avoid more'.

When you've finished, check:

☐ Tenses — double check that you've used the right tenses.

☐ Agreements — do all the verbs have the correct agreement?

 ☐  ☐  ☐ **Section 5 — Lifestyle and Social & Global Issues**

# Problems in Society

**Q1** Complete the sentences using the imperfect tense of the verb in brackets.
The first one has been done for you. Then translate the sentences into **English**.

a) Los optimistas todavía ......**pensaban**...... que no habría guerra. **(pensar)**

b) Los más necesitados ........................ en alojamiento <u>temporal</u>. **(vivir)**

This is the opposite of 'permanente'.

c) Nosotros ........................ la violencia de primera mano. **(ver)**

d) La injusticia ........................ peor que el año anterior. **(ser)**

**Q2** Translate the sentences below into **English**. Before you start, think carefully
about whether you'll need to include the articles in your translations.

a) El racismo y la desigualdad no tienen sitio en la sociedad actual.

b) Podríamos construir hogares para la gente que los necesita.

Articles are words like 'the' and 'a'.

c) Creo que el gobierno debe hacer más para ayudar a los "sin techo".

d) La guerra destruye las comunidades y causa la pobreza.

**Q3** Translate the superlative phrases in bold into **Spanish**. The first
one has been done for you. Then translate the whole sentence.

Make sure your answers agree with the appropriate nouns.

a) The level of crime in my city is **the lowest** in England. ➡ ......**el más bajo**......

b) Of all society's problems, poverty is **one of the worst**. ➡ ...........................

c) The level of unemployment is **the highest** in Europe. ➡ ...........................

d) This year, the charity's campaign is **one of the best**. ➡ ...........................

**Q4** Translate the following passage into **Spanish**.

Q2 will give you a hint on how to translate this.

> I think that achieving equality is the biggest problem in <u>today's society</u>.
> It is easy to avoid this problem, but it is important that we fight against
> prejudice. I believe that it is everyone's responsibility <u>to campaign</u> for
> equality. I hope that the government listens and does something.

Use a construction with 'hacer' to translate this.

When you've finished, check:

☐ Articles — have you used the correct articles and agreements?

☐ Triggers — have you spotted all the phrases that trigger certain tenses?

Section 5 — Lifestyle and Social & Global Issues

# Contributing to Society

**Q1** Translate the impersonal constructions in bold into **English**, using either 'one' or 'it' as the subject. The first one has been done for you. Then translate the sentences.

a) **Hay que** reciclar para ayudar al medio ambiente. ⟹ ........**One has to**........

b) **Parece que** alguna gente requiere más apoyo que otra. ⟹ ...............................

c) **Se tiene que** proteger a la gente vulnerable. ⟹ ...............................

d) **Se dice que** cambiar a la energía renovable es fácil. ⟹ ...............................

**Q2** Translate these comments about recycling into **Spanish**.

a) I always try to reuse lots of plastic.

b) They used to separate glass, plastic and cardboard.

c) We organised the rubbish every day because recycling is important.

d) Javi used to compost* his food waste.
    *to compost = convertir en abono

*Trips to the tip were always a barrel of laughs.*

**Q3** Translate this passage into **Spanish**. Before you start, answer the questions below.

> My aunt works for a charity that looks after the poorest people from all around the world. She fights for the human rights of those affected or threatened by hunger and war. I really admire her for helping them and hope that one day <u>I can</u> help too.

a) How will you translate 'the poorest people'? ...............................

b) How do you say 'those affected' in Spanish? ...............................

c) Which tense will you need to use for the underlined phrase? ...............................

**Q4** Rosa is talking about her friend. Translate the following passage into **English**.

> Cada sábado, mi amiga trabaja como voluntaria en <u>una residencia para ancianos</u>. A mí no me gustaría porque tiene que cocinar, pero a ella le encanta preparar y servir la comida a toda la gente que vive allí. Ha ayudado a otros desde una edad muy joven y cuando sea mayor, quiere trabajar como enfermera.

Break this down to help you translate it.

Before you start, think about:

☐ Tenses — can you recognise which tenses are used in the passage?

☐ Flow — will you need to rearrange any sentences to make your translation sound natural in English?

# Global Events

**Q1** Tick the sentences below in which the words in bold will be translated using 'ser'. Then translate the sentences into **Spanish**.

a) The athlete **was** ill before the Olympic Games. ☐

b) Drinking water for everyone **is** what the government wants. ☐

c) Volunteer work **will be** compulsory in schools within ten years. ☐

d) The charities **are** working in difficult conditions. ☐

e) They **are** happy with the security for the World Cup. ☐

**Q2** Complete the Spanish sentences with the pluperfect 'they' form of the verb in brackets. The first one has been done for you. Then translate the sentences into **English**.

a) ......**Habían empezado**...... la guerra sin considerar las consecuencias. **(empezar)**

b) Demasiadas personas ya ................................................... . **(morir)**

c) ................................................... todo en el terremoto. **(perder)**

⟋Q1 will help you with this.

d) ................................................... mucho del <u>Mundial</u> antes de irse. **(hablar)**

**Q3** The couples below are talking about what they've seen in the news. Translate their dialogue into **Spanish**.

↘This 'the' isn't translated into Spanish.

a) **Diego:** Last week, there was a protest* <u>in the name of</u> equality.

   **Elena:** It is a shame that it is still such a big problem worldwide.

b) **Paula:** Next year, there will be an international music festival in our town.

   **Alexa:** Many people campaigned to have it here.

c) **Emma:** The law is changing so that hypermarkets can sell more fair trade products.

   **Chloe:** Yes I heard about that. The change will benefit many people.

   *a protest = una manifestación

**Q4** Translate the following passage into **English**.

You can write this in numbers in your translation.

> Empezando en el año <u>mil novecientos nueve</u>, el Día Internacional de la Mujer se celebra cada año el ocho de marzo. El día celebra los éxitos sociales, económicos, políticos y culturales de las mujeres. La desigualdad de <u>género</u> existe todavía pero ← esperamos que llegue un día en que dejará de existir.

When you've finished, check:

☐ Word order — do you need to rearrange any sentences to make them sound natural in English?

☐ Tenses — have you translated the different tenses correctly?

Use the context of the passage to help you translate this.

☹ ☐   ☺ ☐   ☺ ☐

# Mixed Practice

**Q1** Translate these statements into **English**.

**a)** El terremoto del año pasado dejó a mucha gente sin hogar.

**b)** Debido a campañas mundiales, la velocidad de la deforestación ha desacelerado.

**c)** Hubo unas inundaciones terribles que crearon mucha pobreza.

**d)** La organización benéfica intenta solucionar los problemas ambientales del mundo.

**Q2** Carmen is talking about her sleeping habits. Translate the passage below into **Spanish**.

I used to sleep really well because I lived in the country and it was quiet there. I live in the city now and there is a lot of traffic at night. I try to go to bed early but it is difficult to sleep because of the noise pollution. I'm always tired.

Traffic always made Jeffrey a bit ant-sy.

**Q3** Translate these sentences into **Spanish**.

**a)** My mum never eats junk food, but she never exercises either.

**b)** He used to get drunk a lot but now he is very healthy and runs four times a week.

**c)** My sister wants to stop smoking because she wants to run a marathon.

**d)** I couldn't sleep but the doctor gave me some pills* and I don't have problems any more.
*a pill = una pastilla

**Q4** The people below are talking about how they make a difference in their towns. Translate their dialogues into **English**.

**a)** **José:** ¿Todavía trabajas en la tienda solidaria los fines de semana?

**Sami:** Desafortunadamente, la tienda fue destruida por el huracán del mes pasado.

**b)** **Luisa:** Mañana, voy a recoger todo el plástico del parque del barrio.

**Toma:** Creo que despertará consciencia sobre el problema del plástico.

**c)** **Katya:** Voy a comprar un coche eléctrico. Será mejor para el medio ambiente.

**Sofía:** Su desarrollo es muy importante para reducir los niveles de contaminación.

# Mixed Practice

**Q5**    Traduce las frases siguientes al **inglés**.

  **a)**  Muchos niños sufren problemas debido a los niveles de polución altos.

  **b)**  Mi amiga se cayó y se rompió la pierna cuando el terremoto destruyó su casa.

  **c)**  Muchas personas se enfermaron después de las inundaciones del año pasado.

  **d)**  A algunas mujeres les preocupan que los gases de escape dañen a sus bebés.

  **e)**  Es fácil quemarse* porque la capa de ozono es muy delgada.
    *quemarse = to get sunburnt

**Q6**    Traduce el texto siguiente al **español**.

> Five years ago, I didn't have a job and I was homeless.
> A local charity helped me to find a job.  I was lucky because
> the people who worked there gave me a lot of support.  In
> the future, I would like to volunteer in order to help others.

Don't forget that in Spanish you 'have' luck.

**Q7**    Read the following conversations between Juan and Nico.  Translate their dialogue into **Spanish**.

  **a)**  **Juan:**   The World Cup will create many jobs and it will lower unemployment.
      **Nico:**   It will only help temporarily though.  People won't have jobs when it finishes.

  **b)**  **Juan:**   I'm going to work at a music festival in August.  Do you want to come?
      **Nico:**   I can't because I'll be working as a volunteer with a children's charity.

  **c)**  **Juan:**   Did you see the concert in Mexico that those celebrities organised for charity?
      **Nico:**   Yes, I watched it on TV.  I gave money to the charity afterwards.

**Q8**    Translate the text below into **English**.

> Para la gente que vive en pobreza, puede ser difícil vivir una vida sana.
> A menudo, la comida que contiene mucho azúcar o sal es más barata
> que las opciones más sanas.  Eso significa que es difícil para la gente
> con poco dinero obtener el alimento* que necesita de su comida.

  *el alimento = nourishment

# Mixed Practice

**Q9**  Mikael is discussing an article he read in the paper.
Translate his ideas into **English**.

> El gobierno quiere que la gente vaya más en bici y ande en vez de conducir.  Sería mejor para el medio ambiente.  Me parece bien que el gobierno lo piense, pero no creo que sea el problema más importante.  Deberíamos dar más ayuda a los que la necesitan en nuestra sociedad.

**Q10**  Read the following conversation between Kris and Coral.  Translate their dialogue into **Spanish**.

The two sisters had quite different feelings about Inma's chocolate allergy.

a)  **Kris:**  Would you like to try a piece of this chocolate cake?
   **Coral:**  I would love to but I can't eat chocolate anymore.
   I've discovered that I'm allergic* to milk.

b)  **Kris:**  Have you had to change your diet?
   **Coral:**  Yes, but now I find it easier to eat more healthily.

c)  **Kris:**  That's great, do you have more energy now?
   **Coral:**  Yes, and I feel much healthier.
   *allergic = alérgico/a

**Q11**  Translate the following statements about renewable energy and technology into **English**.

a)  Es importante que reduzcamos las emisiones.  Debemos usar más energía renovable en nuestra sociedad, por ejemplo el uso de electricidad para alimentar los coches.

b)  Sin embargo, la tecnología es bastante cara todavía, lo que excluye a mucha gente.  No me parece que sea accesible a todas las partes de la sociedad.

**Q12**  Traduce el texto siguiente al **español**.   Use the correct form of 'acabar de' to translate this.

> A new food shop <u>has just</u> opened near my house.  In the shop, there are big containers of food.  People can use them to fill their own jars and bags.  The shop also believes in giving people fair opportunities.  It employs lots of people who have had difficulties finding work because of their disabilities*.

*a disability = una incapacidad

Section 5 — Lifestyle and Social & Global Issues

# Where to Go

**Q1**    Translate these sentences into **English**. Before you start, <u>underline</u> all the verbs. The first one has been done for you.

     **a)**    <u>Fui</u> de vacaciones a Francia.

     **b)**    ¿Adónde irás el año próximo?

     **c)**    Prefieren ir de vacaciones al extranjero.

     **d)**    Nos quedaremos algunas noches en Madrid.

**Q2**    Translate the question words in bold into **Spanish**. The first one has been done for you. Then translate the whole sentence using the 'vosotros' form.

     **a)**    **When** are you going to return to Greece?   ➡   **Cuándo** ....................

     **b)**    **Where** do you want to go on holiday this year?   ➡   ....................

     **c)**    **How many** days did you spend in the United States?   ➡   ....................

     **d)**    **Which** country is your favourite?   ➡   ....................

> Remember to think about the word order of your questions.

**Q3**    Translate these sentences into **English**. Before you start, think carefully about how to translate each of the phrases in bold.

     **a)**    **El año pasado**, pasó tiempo en Escocia con su padrastro.

     **b)**    Voy a quedarme en el sur de Alemania **este verano**.

     **c)**    Quieren regresar a Italia **el julio que viene** para ver a sus amigos.

     **d)**    **En el futuro**, me gustaría visitar a mi familia en Gales.

Maria couldn't contain her excitement when she found out she was going camping in Scotland.

**Q4**    Translate the following passage into **Spanish**.

> This set phrase uses the verb 'tener'.

> I would like to go abroad every year, but it's very expensive. <u>We are lucky</u> because my grandparents live in Spain, so we can stay with them.

**Q5**    Traduce la conversación entre Alma y Javier al **inglés**.

     **a)**   **Alma:**    Javier, ¿vas de vacaciones con tus padres? Me han dicho que van a Japón.
            **Javier:**    Sí, vamos por dos semanas y queremos visitar Tokyo.

     **b)**   **Alma:**    ¡Qué suerte! Iré a Japón el año que viene con mi novia.
            **Javier:**    ¿Qué querríais hacer allí? <u>Tengo muchas ganas</u> de ir a Japón.

> This is another set phrase, similar to the one in Q4.

     **c)**   **Alma:**    Quiero ir a los museos de Tokyo. Me interesa la cultura japonesa.
            **Javier:**    Te contaré todo de nuestro viaje cuando regresemos.

# Accommodation

**Q1** Translate these sentences into **Spanish**. Before you start, <u>underline</u> the adjectives in each sentence. The first one has been done for you.

*Think about your word order — remember that not all adjectives go after the noun they describe.*

   **a)** This hotel has <u>excellent</u> facilities.

   **b)** I'm looking for accommodation with a big swimming pool.

   **c)** There is another hotel with air conditioning.

   **d)** The boarding house always has clean sheets*.
     *sheet = la sábana

**Q2** Translate these sentences into **English**. Before you start, think carefully about how you will translate the conditional verbs in bold.

   **a)** Si todavía hay habitaciones disponibles en la pensión, **me gustaría** una habitación doble.

   **b)** Mañana **podríamos** quedarnos en el albergue juvenil.

   **c)** Pienso que media pensión **sería** lo mejor.

   **d)** **Deberías** <u>telefonear</u> al hotel para hacer la reserva.

*Think about how to translate 'telefonear' so it sounds natural in English.*

**Q3** Translate the comparisons in bold into **Spanish**. Then translate the whole sentence. The first one has been done for you.

   **a)** Youth hostels **are more interesting than** hotels. ➡ ..... **son más interesantes que** .....

   **b)** It is **more expensive** to stay in a luxury hotel. ➡ ...................................................

   **c)** Camping is **as fun as** going on a cruise. ➡ ...................................................

   **d)** A tent is **less comfortable than** a state-owned hotel. ➡ ...................................................

   **e)** This room is **more modern than** <u>that one</u>. ➡ ...................................................

*Think carefully about which pronoun you need here — there are two correct options.*

**Q4** Traduce el texto siguiente al **inglés**.

> Cuando vamos de vacaciones, solemos ir de camping. Pienso que es mejor que alojarse en un hotel porque los campings cuestan mucho menos que los hoteles y suelen tener muy buenas instalaciones. Por ejemplo, un camping que visité el año pasado tenía una piscina y estaba situado al lado de la playa.

When you've finished, check:

☐ Subject — are the subjects of your verbs consistent?

☐ Comparatives — have you translated the comparisons correctly?

# Getting Ready

**Q1** Translate these sentences into **Spanish**. Before you start, <u>underline</u> the subject of the verb. The first one has been done for you.

**a)** <u>Jo</u> wanted to make a reservation.    **c)** We would like a map of the city.

**b)** The room has sea views.    **d)** Will the hotel have any single rooms available?

**Q2** Translate the sentences below into **Spanish**. Before you start, think about how you would translate the phrases in bold.

**a)** **For me**, it's important to learn the local language before travelling abroad.

**b)** I don't want to visit the museum **without him**.

**c)** Gabriel, are you going to take your guidebook **with you**?

**Q3** Complete the Spanish sentences with the correct present subjunctive form of the verb in brackets. Then translate the sentences into **English**. The first one has been done for you.

**a)** Es importante que ......**hagas**...... tu maleta algunos días antes de tu viaje.    **(hacer)**

**b)** Espero que el parador ..................... habitaciones con vistas a las montañas.    **(tener)**

**c)** Voy a hablar con ellos cuando ..................... al hotel.    **(llegar)**

**d)** No creo que <u>Las Alas de Hada</u> ..................... el mejor hotel de la ciudad.    **(ser)**
— You don't need to translate this name.

**Q4** Traduce el texto siguiente al **inglés**.

> Me encanta sacar fotos cuando visito nuevos lugares.
> El año pasado fui a India y un mono* me robó la máquina.
> Necesito comprar una nueva antes de ir a África en agosto.

*el mono = the monkey

**Q5** Translate the conversation between Inma and Paula into **Spanish**.

**a)** **Inma:** Are you looking forward to your holiday?
**Paula:** Yes, but I have a thousand things to do before going away.

**b)** **Inma:** What do you have to do? You've still got a lot of time.
**Paula:** I need to <u>apply for</u> a new passport.
— You'll need to use the verb 'solicitar' here.

**c)** **Inma:** You should sort that out soon. I had to wait two months for mine.
**Paula:** I'll do it in the morning.

Section 6 — Travel and Tourism

# Getting There

**Q1**  Translate these sentences into **Spanish**. Before you start, underline the adverb of place in each sentence. The first one has been done for you.

**a)**  The service station was <u>far away</u>.

**b)**  Is there an underground station here?

**c)**  Jo likes to drive everywhere.

**d)**  They travelled there by aeroplane. ◤

There is more than one way to translate the adverb of place in this sentence.

**Q2**  Identify the tense used for the verb in bold in each sentence. Then translate the sentences into **English**. The first one has been done for you.

**a)**  Sus amigos **prefieren** viajar en barco. ▷ ........**present**........

**b)**  El tren a Barcelona **partirá** del andén seis. ▷ ........................

**c)**  **Compré** un billete de ida y vuelta a Madrid. ▷ ........................

**d)**  **Hemos alquilado** el coche por dos semanas. ▷ ........................

Carmen had been hoping for a more modern service for her trip to Madrid.

**Q3**  Translate this passage into **Spanish**. Before you start, answer the questions below.

You'll need to translate this as 'the driver of the bus'.

My flight arrived very late at the airport. The <u>bus driver</u> said there was a traffic jam on the motorway. I decided to catch the train. It was very busy and the journey took three hours. Next time, I will <u>rent a car</u>. ◄

Look back at Q2 for a clue on how to say 'rent a car'.

**a)**  How do you say 'very late' in Spanish? ....................................................

**b)**  How will you translate 'took three hours'? ....................................................

**c)**  Which tense will you need for the final sentence? ....................................................

**Q4**  Translate the following passage into **English**.

Al llegar a la estación más de veinte minutos tarde, me preocupaba llegar tarde a la reunión. Yo estaba en la esquina de la calle al lado de la estación cuando oí mi nombre. Vi a mi compañera, Jenny, quien había reservado un taxi para ir a la reunión. Fui con ella y llegamos <u>a tiempo</u>.

Before you start, think about:

☐  Vocab — are there any words you don't know?

☐  Tenses — do you know which tenses you'll need to use in each sentence?

Think carefully about how to translate this phrase.

# What to Do

**Q1** Translate these sentences into **Spanish**. Before you start, circle the verbs that you will translate using the infinitive. The first one has been done for you.

    **a)** What do you like (to do) on holiday?    **c)** You can see more of the city on foot.

    **b)** My mum likes visiting the theme park.    **d)** I love going to the beach.

**Q2** Complete the Spanish sentences with the correct article, then translate the sentences into **English**. The first one has been done for you.

    **a)** Juan nadaría en ....**el**.... mar a diario pero ............ agua está fría.

    **b)** Quiero ver ............ fotos en ............ galería de arte.

    **c)** Me encanta pasar ............ día tomando ............ sol.

    **d)** <u>Compramos</u> ............ recuerdo en ............ parque de atracciones.

          ↖ Translate this into the past tense.

Ellen wasn't sure if her hat was
big enough to keep off the sun.

**Q3** Translate the phrases in bold into **Spanish** using the present continuous tense. The first one has been done for you. Then translate each sentence.

    **a)** **We are thinking** about going horse riding. ▷ ............ **Estamos pensando** ............

    **b)** My parents **are taking** photos of the castle. ▷ ............................................

    **c)** **I am sending** a postcard to my mum. ▷ ............................................

    **d)** **Are you buying** a ticket before <u>travelling</u>? ▷ ............................................

                 ↖ You'll need to use the infinitive of this verb.

**Q4** Fill in the gaps in **Spanish** in the passage below to complete the translation.

> My family and I <u>are trying</u> to decide where to go on holiday next ◀─ Look back at Q3
> year. My brother wants to go to Wales because he likes surfing.   for a clue on which
> My dad loves visiting cities. I don't really care where we go.   tense to use for the
>                                               underlined phrase.

Mi familia y yo ................................................ decidir adónde ir de

vacaciones el año que viene. Mi hermano quiere ir a Gales porque

................................................ . A mi padre ................................................

las ciudades. A mí ................................................ adónde vamos.

**Q5** Translate these sentences into **English**. Before you start, underline all of the verbs in the preterite tense. The first one has been done for you.

a) <u>Hice</u> muchos deportes acuáticos cuando estaba en Málaga.

b) Vamos a jugar al baloncesto con los chicos de Inglaterra que conocimos ayer.

c) Tuvieron demasiado miedo de hacer deportes de riesgo.

d) ¿Viste una actuación cuando estabas en Londres?

e) Mi hermana me prometió que podríamos hacer alpinismo.

**Q6** Translate the negative phrases in bold into **Spanish**. The first one has been done for you. Then translate each sentence.

*Translate all of these sentences using a double negative in Spanish.*

a) **Nobody was** at the museum. ➡ ............**No estaba nadie**............

b) **We never buy** souvenirs. ➡ ............................................

c) **There is nothing** else to do. ➡ ............................................

d) **There's not a single place\* left** on the trip. ➡ ............................................
   *\*place = una plaza*

**Q7** Translate the conversation between Claudia and Pedro into **English**.

a) **Claudia:** Hola, Pedro. ¿Estás disfrutando de las vacaciones?
   **Pedro:** Sí. Hoy, <u>fui</u> al monumento, y mañana voy a ver las ruinas del castillo. ¿Quieres venir conmigo? — Look back at Q5 for a clue on which tense this is.

b) **Claudia:** No puedo. Ya tengo planes. Voy de compras para buscar recuerdos.
   **Pedro:** ¿A qué hora vas? ¿Quieres almorzar juntos? Comeré a las dos.

c) **Claudia:** Sí, me encantaría. Quiero probar la comida de esta región. Parece muy rica.
   **Pedro:** Sí, ¡tengo muchas ganas de probar los dulces!

**Q8** Traduce el texto siguiente al **inglés**.

> Mis vacaciones ideales serían en un país donde se pueda esquiar por las mañanas y relajarse en la playa por las tardes. He oído que esto es posible en Norteamérica y en partes de España. Para mí, es más divertido hacer algo activo que tomar el sol todo el día.

When you've finished, check:

☐ Flow — does it make sense in English?

☐ Verbs — have you translated the verbs correctly?

Section 6 — Travel and Tourism

# Practical Stuff

**Q1**  Translate these questions into **Spanish** using the 'usted' form of the verb.

   **a)**  Please can you help me?

   **b)**  Have you lost your purse?

   **c)**  Do you have a map I can borrow?

   **d)**  Can you take me to the garage to pick up my car?

   **e)**  Have you seen a police station near here?

   **f)**  Do you know where I can validate my ticket?

**Q2**  Complete the Spanish sentences using the perfect tense form of the verb in brackets.  Then translate the sentences into **English**.

> Think about how to translate this verb — 'perder' has several meanings.

   **a)**  Nosotros ............**hemos perdido**............ el tren.  **(perder)**

   **b)**  Ella ..................................... la maleta en el tranvía.  **(dejar)**

   **c)**  Ellos me ..................................... el móvil.  **(robar)**

   **d)**  ¿ ..................................... tu billete?  **(encontrar)**

**Q3**  Translate the following conversations into **English**.

   **a)**  **Manni:**  ¿Qué te pasó <u>en el brazo</u>?  ← Think about a natural way to translate this.
   **Laura:**  Tuve un accidente de coche en las vacaciones y me lo rompí.

   **b)**  **Greg:**  Nuestras vacaciones fueron terribles.  El hotel estaba muy sucio.
   **Paul:**  ¡Qué pena!  Deberías quejarte a la compañía.

   **c)**  **Victor:**  Camarera, perdón, ¿tiene usted una mesa para dos disponible?
   **Sophie:**  Sí, pero hay <u>un período de espera</u> de una hora.  ¿Quieren esperar?
   └ Think about the meaning of 'espera' to help you translate this set phrase.

**Q4**  Translate the following passage into **Spanish**.

> Don't translate the underlined place names.

> In April, we went on holiday to Spain.  We went by boat from <u>Portsmouth</u> to <u>Santander</u> because we wanted to take our car.  We arrived in Spain at rush hour, and the roads were very busy.  Someone tried to overtake us and my dad had to brake quickly.  We were lucky because there wasn't an accident!

Bianca took matters into her own hands when the traffic got too much.

When you've finished, check:

   ☐  Person — have you used the correct person of each verb?

   ☐  Subject — have you used the correct form of the verb for the subject?

  ☐    ☐  ☺  ☐

# Mixed Practice

**Q1** Translate the following sentences into **Spanish**.

**a)** It was really hot in Spain, so we did water sports everyday.

**b)** When she went to Wales, Emily was too scared to go horse riding.

**c)** I would like to try skiing <u>when I visit</u> France next year.

**d)** When he went to London, he saw a lot of the city and visited lots of monuments.

**e)** I rented a car when I went to Denmark, so I had to take my driving licence with me.

**f)** She's looking forward to trying the local food <u>when she goes</u> to Pakistan.

*Which tense follows 'cuando' when the action hasn't happened yet?*

**Q2** Translate these sentences into **English**.

**a)** Annika no pudo ir al parque de atracciones porque había olvidado su monedero.

**b)** Tuvimos suerte porque no había atascos en la autopista.

**c)** No puede ir de vacaciones este año porque su madre se ha roto la pierna.

**d)** Desafortunadamente, el hotel cometió un error y canceló nuestra reserva.

**e)** La camarera nos hizo un descuento en la cuenta porque tuvimos muchos problemas.

**Q3** María is talking about what she likes to do on holiday. Translate what she says into **English**.

> Cuando voy de vacaciones, doy paseos por la ciudad cada día. Lo que me gusta hacer es ir a las ruinas de castillos.  Este año voy a Bilbao, y voy a visitar uno de los castillos más viejos de España. He comprado una máquina nueva para sacar muchas fotos.

**Q4** Traduce el texto siguiente al **español**.

> I would love to go on holiday abroad, but it's too expensive.  However, there are many fun activities that you can do here in the UK.  I like going camping, but my sleeping bag isn't very comfortable.  When I'm older, I hope that I have enough money to stay in hotels.

*Which tenses should you use for the last sentence?*

# Mixed Practice

**Q5** Read the following conversation between Sonia and Tony.
Translate their dialogue into **English**.

**a)** **Sonia:** ¿Has ido a Holanda? Iré en barco desde Hull en el verano.

**Tony:** Sí, fui allí hace algunos años. ¿A qué parte vas?

**b)** **Sonia:** Vamos a Amsterdam. Nos quedamos tres noches en total.

**Tony:** He visitado Amsterdam y hay muchos museos y galerías de arte.

**c)** **Sonia:** No me interesa ir a museos ni galerías. ¿Qué más hay que hacer?

**Tony:** Podrías alquilar una bicicleta. Es una buena manera de ver la ciudad.

**Q6** Translate these sentences into **Spanish**.

**a)** They won't spend much time at the youth hostel because there are lots of things to do.

**b)** I want to eat at local restaurants, so it would be better for us to stay half board.

**c)** We want a hotel with a swimming pool so that the children can go swimming.

**d)** I prefer staying in hotel rooms with a balcony with a view of the sea.

**e)** He doesn't like travelling by plane, so he normally drives to Portugal.

**Q7** Translate the passage below into **English**.

> Desafortunadamente, mi regreso a Inglaterra la semana pasada
> fue un desastre. Me perdí durante el camino al aeropuerto y
> tuve que preguntar direcciones varias veces. Al llegar tarde
> al aeropuerto, descubrí que se había cancelado el vuelo. La
> próxima vez viajaré en barco. ¡Será mucho más fácil que <u>volar</u>!

Think about the meaning of 'el
vuelo' in order to translate 'volar'.

**Q8** Marcus is talking about where he went on holiday
last year. Translate the passage into **Spanish**.

> Last year, I spent my holidays travelling through Europe by train. It was a fantastic
> trip because I find the railway really interesting. The views of the mountain ranges
> from the train were beautiful. The only difficulty was that I speak neither French
> nor German, so it was sometimes hard to find the platform for the next train.

# Mixed Practice

**Q9** Translate these sentences into **English**.

a) Quisiéramos quedarnos en Berlín, pero ninguno de los hoteles tiene habitaciones disponibles.

b) Hará mucho calor en Australia, así que reservaré una habitación con aire acondicionado.

c) El hotel es famoso por su comida, y por esta razón elegí quedarme en pensión completa.

Robert didn't have the heart to tell Jenny he wasn't a fan of the local food.

**Q10** Translate the following conversation between Kyle and José in a travel agents into **Spanish**. It's a formal conversation so think about which 'you' form to use.

a) **Kyle:** Hello, I'd like to book a hotel room for my holiday. Can you help me?
   **José:** Of course. Where would you like to go?

b) **Kyle:** I want to go to a hot country. I would love to relax by the pool all day.
   **José:** There are lots of hotels with big swimming pools in Italy.
   Would you like to go there?

c) **Kyle:** Yes, I've never been to Italy.
   **José:** I've found a hotel with a room available near Rome.
   I'll make a reservation for you.

**Q11** Translate the following passage into **Spanish**.

> During my gap year I travelled to lots of countries, but I never visited South America. When I'm older, I would like to go to Peru. I would stay with my friend who lives in Lima. I would like to visit her because <u>I haven't seen her for two years</u>.

Think carefully about word order in this phrase.

**Q12** Traduce el texto siguiente al **inglés**.

> El año pasado, fui a Nueva Zelanda*. Me quedé en unos albergues juveniles y fue muy divertido. Viajé en transporte público pero lo encontré difícil porque los autobuses siempre llegaban tarde. La próxima vez, alquilaré un coche para poder visitar los lugares más remotos. Todavía me quedan muchos sitios que visitar.

*Nueva Zelanda = New Zealand

Section 6 — Travel and Tourism

# School Life

**Q1**    Translate these sentences into **Spanish**.  Before you start,
think carefully about how to translate the time expressions.

Nancy felt like she spent
her whole life in school.

    **a)**   They have P.E. before lunch, at <u>one o'clock</u>. ← You only need the single
                                                               article for 'one o'clock'.

    **b)**   I have a snack in the afternoon, at two thirty.

    **c)**   We have break from half past ten to quarter to eleven.

    **d)**   The state school finishes at twenty five past three.

    **e)**   Ten past nine is too early for maths class.

**Q2**    Complete the sentences below using the correct pronoun for the nouns in brackets.
The first one has been done for you.  Then translate the sentences into **English**.

    **a)**   ....**Lo**.... odio porque es aburrido y no saco buenas notas.       **(el comercio)**

    **b)**   El lunes pasado, ............ dejé en el autobús.              **(mi mochila)**

    **c)**   Siempre ........... ayudan con los deberes.      Think carefully    **(yo)**
                                                   about this one.

    **d)**   Ellos ........... decoraron con banderas de España y mapas del país.   **(el aula)**

**Q3**    Put a tick (✓) next to the school rules that say what pupils should do and a
cross (x) next to the ones they shouldn't.  Then translate the rules into **English**.

    **a)**   Hay que llegar a tiempo.              □

    **b)**   Se debe llevar el uniforme correcto.     □       Think about how you can

    **c)**   Está prohibido usar los móviles en el colegio.     □    reflect the formal language of
                                                      these rules in your translation.

    **d)**   No se puede hablar en la biblioteca.     □

    **e)**   Muestren respeto a otras personas.      □

**Q4**    Read this extract, then fill in the gaps with words in **Spanish** to complete the translation.

> Our school doesn't accept bullying.  The teachers are very understanding
> and they always listen to us.  If <u>you</u> feel threatened by other pupils, don't
> be afraid because there are lots of people who can help <u>you</u>.

Use the singular,
informal 'you' in
your translation.

Nuestro instituto no acepta ....................... . Los profesores son muy ..................................

y siempre nos escuchan.  Si ............................................................. por otros estudiantes,

........................................... porque hay mucha gente que ................................................. .

**Q5**  Translate the comparisons in bold into **Spanish**. The first one has been done for you. Then translate the rest of the sentence.

a)  The dining room is **newer than** the classrooms. ⇨ .............................**más nuevo que**.............................

b)  The religious school is **as big as** the private school. ⇨ .......................................................

c)  The changing rooms are **noisier than** the library. ⇨ .......................................................

d)  Today, the workshop is **as cold as** the gym. ⇨ .......................................................

**Q6**  Translate these sentences into **English**. Before you start, circle the verbs in the pluperfect tense, and underline the verbs in the perfect tense. The first one has been done for you.

a)  Olivia y Tom (habían olvidado) sus libros de geografía.

b)  José y yo no habíamos hecho los deberes para nuestra clase de latín.

c)  He perdido mi boli y no tengo otro para el examen de mañana.

d)  Jaime ha comprado lápices de colores para su clase de arte.

e)  No pudimos hacer la actividad porque la pizarra interactiva se había roto.

**Q7**  Translate the following passage into **Spanish**.

During break, we usually chat, but yesterday we went to the library to finish our maths homework. Sometimes, we go to the canteen. In summer, we play football on the field or we relax in the playground*, but in winter, we prefer to stay in the classroom.

*playground = el patio

When you've finished, check:

☐ Word order — does your translation sound natural in Spanish?

☐ Reflexive verbs — have you spotted them all?

**Q8**  Read the following conversation between Pablo and Ana. Translate their dialogue into **English**.

a)  **Pablo:**  Estoy muy estresado por los exámenes.
     Mis padres quieren que saque buenas notas.
    **Ana:**  He leído un artículo sobre cómo bajar los niveles de estrés durante los exámenes.

b)  **Pablo:**  ¿Aprendiste algo útil?
    **Ana:**  Leí que es importante relajarte.
                                    — Q5 will help you with this comparison.
c)  **Pablo:**  Es <u>más difícil que</u> parece. Tengo que repasar mucho para no suspender.
    **Ana:**  No tienes que preocuparte. Sé que vas a aprobar.

# School Events

**Q1** Translate these sentences into **Spanish**. Before you start, translate the quantifiers in bold. The first one has been done for you.

> ⎧ Make sure your answers agree with the nouns in the sentence. ⎫

a) We have **too many** tests in class. ▷ ............. **demasiadas** .............

b) The orchestra <u>puts on</u> **a lot of** shows. ▷ ........................................
  ↖ Translate 'puts on' as 'does' here.

c) There are only **a few** days left of the school year. ▷ ..................................

d) There are **so many** adverts in the school newspaper. ▷ ..................................

**Q2** Translate these passive sentences in the future tense into **English**. Before you start, underline the passive constructions in each one. The first one has been done for you.

a) Todas las clases <u>serán canceladas</u> el martes.

b) El documental será mostrado en el club de películas el jueves.

> ⎧ The passive is formed using 'ser' and the past participle. ⎫

c) La excursión será organizada por los estudiantes.

d) El ensayo* del coro será cambiado desde el lunes al miércoles.
  *el ensayo = practice

**Q3** Translate this passage into **Spanish**.
Before you start, answer the questions below.

> Every year there is a trip abroad with the languages department. Last year, we went to Spain and it was a good opportunity to practise Spanish. Next year, the teachers want to visit France. <u>I have never</u> visited France before. ◀
>
> Use a double negative in your translation.

a) Which tense will you use for 'we went'? ...........................................

b) How will you translate 'a good opportunity'? ...........................................

c) Which word will you use for 'never'? ...........................................

**Q4** Translate the following passage into **English**.

> La reunión de padres tendrá lugar en octubre. Después de la última reunión, mis padres se enfadaron porque mis profesores dijeron que no me esforzaba. Desde entonces he prestado atención durante las clases. El jueves pasado, tuvimos una <u>entrega de premios</u>, y gané un premio. Mis padres están muy orgullosos de mí.
>
> In this context, the verb 'entregar' means the same as 'dar'.

# Education Post-16

**Q1** These students are talking about their hopes for the future. Complete the sentences with the conditional form of the verb in brackets. Then translate the sentences into **English**.

a) **Fred:** Después del bachillerato, me ......**gustaría**...... tomar un año libre. **(gustar)**

b) **Chloe:** Me ...................... trabajar unos meses para ganar dinero. **(encantar)**

c) **Lucía:** En un mundo ideal, ...................... por Europa con una amiga. **(viajar)**

d) **John:** Si tuviera el dinero, ...................... derecho en la universidad. **(estudiar)**

**Q2** Translate these 'if' sentences into **Spanish**. You'll need to use two tenses for each one.

a) If I fail my exams, I will try again next year.

b) I will train to be a programmer if I get good marks in ICT.

c) If I pass my Spanish exam, I will study it at A-level.

d) My parents will be angry <u>with me</u> if I don't make an effort*.
   \* to make an effort = esforzarse ◄— This is one word in Spanish.

George had been wrestling with his ICT homework all morning.

**Q3** Translate Kiara's conversation with her careers advisor, Elías, into **Spanish**. Elías will use the 'tú' form to talk to Kiara because he is older than her.

a) **Elías:** What will you do when you finish your studies? ◄— Which tense does this trigger?
   **Kiara:** I don't know if I will do an apprenticeship or continue with my studies in school.

b) **Elías:** Do you know what type of job you <u>would like</u> to do in the future?
   **Kiara:** I would like to be a gardener. I want to work in the open air.
   Q1 will help you with this tense.

c) **Elías:** It would be useful to do a work experience placement.
   **Kiara:** I think that's a good idea.

**Q4** Translate the following passage into **English**.

El año pasado hice mi experiencia laboral en una fábrica de coches. Me gustó porque quiero llegar a ser ingeniero y el trabajo era interesante. Sin embargo, la fábrica se cerró hace dos meses así que no puedo volver a trabajar allí cuando termine mis estudios. Es <u>una lástima</u> porque habría sido mi trabajo ideal.

— This means the same as 'una pena'.

Before you start, check:
- [ ] Word order — will any of the sentences need rearranging to sound natural in English?
- [ ] Tenses — can you identify all the different tenses in the passage, including the tricky ones?

   **Section 7 — Current & Future Study and Employment**

# Languages for the Future

**Q1** Translate these sentences into **Spanish**. Before you start, think carefully about whether you need to use the present tense or the present subjunctive for the verbs in bold.

    **a)** I believe that language teachers **do** an important job.

    **b)** I doubt that Latin **is** useful now.

    **c)** I think that interpreters **have** an interesting job.

    **d)** I don't believe that people **need** to learn languages.

Buster could speak the language so well, the kids never suspected he wasn't local.

**Q2** Translate this passage into **English**. Before you start, answer the questions below.

> Aprender idiomas es ventajoso en la sociedad de hoy.
> No solo te ayudan a mejorar las habilidades de comunicación,
> sino también los idiomas te dan la oportunidad de conocer a
> gente nueva y ver el mundo desde otra perspectiva. <u>Ser capaz de</u>
> comunicarse en otros idiomas es importante en el mundo actual.

This is another way of saying 'poder'.

    **a)** How will you translate 'ventajoso'? ................................................

    **b)** What does the word 'habilidades' mean? ................................................

    **c)** How do you say 'el mundo actual' in English? ................................................

**Q3** Carolina is talking about her job. Translate what she says into **Spanish**.

> I work in a tourist information office and I <u>know how to</u> speak
> several different languages. Tourists find it helpful when I
> can explain something <u>to them</u> in their own language. In my
> opinion, it's important that everyone learns a different language.

Use the verb 'saber' when translating this phrase.

Think carefully about which pronoun to use here.

**Q4** Traduce la conversación siguiente al **inglés**.

    **a)** **Keri:** ¿Qué quieres hacer cuando seas mayor?
          **Sam:** Quiero trabajar en negocios, por eso <u>estoy aprendiendo</u> el japonés.

How will you translate the present continuous?

    **b)** **Keri:** Pienso que el alemán sería mas útil.
          **Sam:** Sí, pero quisiera vivir en Japón en el futuro.

    **c)** **Keri:** Quisiera un trabajo que use mis habilidades con los idiomas.
          **Sam:** <u>Piensa</u> en ser traductora. Puedes ganar dinero por traducir documentos.

Think about how you will translate this imperative.

# Applying for Jobs

**Q1** Translate these sentences into **Spanish**. Before you start, circle all of the adjectives. The first one has been done for you.

**a)** We need (responsible) and self-confident employees.

**b)** He is good at his job because he is organised.
↳ Translate this using a set phrase.

**c)** I want to change my job because the boss is mean.

**d)** She is successful because she is hardworking.

**Q2** Complete the Spanish sentences with the present tense form of the verb in brackets. The first one has been done for you. Then translate the sentences into **English**.

**a)** Es más fácil obtener un trabajo si ustedes ......**tienen**...... experiencia.   **(tener)**

**b)** Si su trabajo está mal pagado, usted ....................... encontrar uno nuevo.   **(poder)**

**c)** Usted ....................... escribir una carta de solicitud.   **(necesitar)**

**d)** Ustedes ....................... hacer un aprendizaje en el verano.   **(deber)**

**Q3** Translate the following job advert into **English**.

> Se buscan camareros o camareras para trabajar en una cafetería concurrida en el centro de la ciudad.
> Se necesitan empleados simpáticos.
> La puntualidad también es importante y no es necesario tener experiencia. Si le interesa, preséntese en el café con su carta de solicitud.

↳ This verb is an imperative plus a pronoun.

When you've finished, check:
☐ Flow — does your translation suit the context?
☐ Impersonal verbs (formed with 'se') — have you translated them all in a way that sounds natural?

**Q4** Read the following job interview between Sara and Nico. Translate their dialogue into **Spanish**. It's a formal conversation so think about which 'you' form to use.

**a)** **Sara:** Hello, I have seen your job advert and I would like to apply for the position of electrician.

**Nico:** Ok, what relevant skills do you have?   Use the correct form of 'acabar de' + infinitive to translate this.

**b)** **Sara:** I have just finished an electrician's qualification.
I also have experience working for my uncle's business.

**Nico:** Very good. I think experience is important.
I will ring you after interviewing the other candidates*.

*candidate = el candidato

     Section 7 — Current & Future Study and Employment

# Career Choices and Ambitions

**Q1**   Complete these sentences using the subjunctive form of the verb in brackets.
Then translate the sentences into **English**. The first one has been done for you.

a)   Mi madre quiere que yo ........**tenga**........ un trabajo que pague bien.   **(tener)**

b)   Es importante que tú ...................... un trabajo que te guste.   **(encontrar)**

c)   Necesitan a alguien que ...................... francés e italiano.   **(saber)**

d)   Espero que ella ...................... feliz en su nuevo trabajo.   **(ser)**

**Q2**   Translate these sentences into **Spanish**. Think carefully about
whether you need to use the article with the job in each sentence.

a)   I want to be a dentist because you can earn a lot of money.

b)   She will be a good teacher because she likes working with children.

c)   Being a doctor is difficult because there is a lot of pressure.

d)   He loves drama and <u>dreams of</u> becoming* a famous actor. ⟵ — Use 'soñar con'
   *to become = llegar a ser                                          to translate this.

**Q3**   Translate these sentences using the conditional tense into **English**.

a)   Ella tiene una personalidad creativa y le gustaría trabajar como diseñadora.

b)   Si no deseas trabajar en una oficina, podrías aprender a ser albañil.

c)   Me encantaría ser bombera porque quiero hacer algo útil.

**Q4**   Translate the following passage into **Spanish**.

Translate this using
the 'impersonal 'se'.

> Helena hopes to become a soldier when she is older. It's not an easy career, but <u>you</u>
> <u>can</u> travel and help other people. <u>You must</u> be very active and hard-working to succeed.

— Use 'hay que' here.

**Q5**   Translate this passage about working in a hairdresser's into **English**.

> Tengo un trabajo a tiempo parcial en una peluquería enfrente
> de mi casa. Trabajo allí desde hace un año y medio.
> Me encanta porque la gente es simpática, pero <u>lo peor</u> es
> que tengo que levantarme temprano los sábados. Quisiera
> ser peluquera en el futuro y tener mi propia empresa.

When you've finished, check:

☐ Word order — does it
read well in English?

☐ False friends — have
you translated specific
vocabulary correctly?

You'll need an extra word to make your English translation sound natural.

# Mixed Practice

**Q1** Translate these sentences into **Spanish**.

a) Before starting a law degree,
you have to study it at A-level.

b) She is going to do an apprenticeship
with a local electrician.

c) My teacher organised my work
experience in a primary school.

d) I'm going to study art because I
want to become a painter.

e) She likes maths so she is going to
work as a cashier in a bank.

f) If you want to be a nurse, you need
to get good grades in science.

**Q2** Toma is looking at the job adverts in the local paper.
Translate the following advert into **English**.

*Which tense will you use
for the verbs in this list?*

> Se necesita una persona mayor de dieciséis años para ayudar
> en un salón de belleza. Las responsabilidades incluirán: <u>ayudar</u>
> a los clientes, <u>contestar</u> el teléfono, <u>organizar</u> citas y <u>preparar</u>
> tratamientos*. Hay que ser puntual y trabajador/a. Interesados
> deben rellenar la solicitud y enviarla por correo electrónico.

It was too late for Jenny to admit
that she had lied about being a
technical whiz on her CV.

*un tratamiento = a treatment

**Q3** Translate these sentences into **English**.

a) En Navidad, nuestro coro va a cantar en el salón del colegio.

b) Mis padres me dieron permiso para hacer la excursión de geografía el miércoles.

c) Si haces una donación mañana, no tendrás que llevar uniforme.

d) Van a vender galletas en la cantina para apoyar a una caridad local.

**Q4** Sofía is talking about her plans for the summer.
Translate what she says into **Spanish**.

> I'm going to the south of Germany soon to work as a
> nanny*. I still haven't met the family, so I'm a little nervous.
> I organised this job <u>through</u> a company that my friend has
> used. I hope to have lots of opportunities to improve my
> German before studying it at university next year.

*Think carefully about
how to translate
'through' in this sentence.*

*nanny = el/la canguro

**Section 7 — Current & Future Study and Employment**

# Mixed Practice

**Q5** Laura is talking about her work experience in London. Translate her comments into **English**.

a) Fui a Londres y cuando estuve allí, organicé alguna experiencia laboral.

b) Conocí a un funcionario local y hablamos en inglés durante la entrevista.

c) Estudié portugués y alemán en la universidad y eso le <u>impresionó</u>. Me ofreció el trabajo.

d) Voy a trabajar en la embajada* española y utilizar mi conocimiento de varias lenguas.
   * la embajada = the embassy

*Use your knowledge of 'impresionante' to work out what this means.*

**Q6** Translate the following passage into **English**.

> La semana pasada algunas personas vinieron al instituto y nos hablaron de sus trabajos. Un cocinero hizo una demostración el martes. Nos mostró cómo preparar una paella, y nos dio información sobre su carrera. Todavía no sé lo que quiero hacer en el futuro. Voy a buscar las opciones de carreras en la red.

**Q7** Translate these people's future plans into **Spanish**.

a) **Mateo:** I would love to take a gap year and travel to Latin America. I would like to work as a volunteer with a charity.

b) **Leon:** I have seen an advert for nurses to work in a local hospital. <u>They are looking</u> for people who <u>have</u> a biology degree. I'm going to apply for the position.

c) **Sara:** When I'm older I want to be a butcher, so <u>I am doing</u> an apprenticeship with a local company. In the future I want to be the boss of my own business.

*You'll need to use the subjunctive here.*

*Use the present, not the present continuous, here.*

**Q8** Translate the following passage into **Spanish**.

> School bullying bothers me because it is very unfair. It's a big problem in schools. In the future I want to be a counsellor* who helps victims of bullying. I'm going to study psychology** at university. I'll need to be patient and listen well to other people.

   * counsellor = el consejero/a   **psychology = la psicología

# Mixed Practice

**Q9**  Translate these sentences into **Spanish**.

**a)**  Last year, I felt a lot of pressure at school.  I worried about failing my exams.  My teachers gave me a lot of support and I passed them.

**b)**  I think French is boring, so I am often absent from class.  My mum wants me to go to class.  She thinks that learning a language is important.

**c)**  I go to a religious school, and R.E. is compulsory.  I would prefer to go to a state school because pupils have more variety in the subjects they study.

**Q10**  Translate the following application letter into **English**.

*(EDEXCEL & EDUQAS)*

> Think about the language you would use to write a formal letter in English.

Estimada Señorita García,

Leí su anuncio que se busca periodista.  Quisiera solicitar el puesto.  Estudio periodismo desde hace tres años y aprobé los exámenes finales de la universidad con resultados excelentes.

No creo que haya una candidata más perfecta porque tengo la experiencia, el entusiasmo y la <u>destreza</u> que se requiere para este trabajo.

Le saluda atentamente*.

Clara Smith

*Le saluda atentamente = Yours sincerely

Clara made sure she always got the best scoop.

This means the same as 'habilidad'.

**Q11**  Several students are talking about their families' jobs. Translate their conversations into **English**.

**a)  Ana:**  Estoy pensando en entrar en el ejército.  ¿Es verdad que tu padre es militar?
  **Karl:**  Era militar hace muchos años, pero ahora es policía.

**b)  Kai:**  ¿Tu hermano todavía quiere ser escritor?  Le interesaba lo que pasaba en el mundo.
  **Luc:**  Sí, es su objetivo.  Ha encontrado un trabajo con el periódico local.

**c)  Tina:**  Mi madre quiere que yo sea enfermera como ella pero quiero viajar.
  **Ali:**  Podrías trabajar como enfermera en el ejército.  Sería muy variado y trabajarías en otros países.

# Answers

*The answers to these questions are sample answers only, just to give you an idea of how they might be translated. There may be different ways to translate the sentences and passages that are also correct.*

## Section 2 — Me, My Family and Friends

### Page 7 — About Yourself

**Q1** a) I am called Ana Luisa.
  b) tiene — My friend is fourteen years old.
  c) es — Luca's birthday is (on) the 20th of May.
  d) sé, escribir — I don't know how to spell / write your surname.

**Q2** a) Mi hermano y yo somos españoles.
  b) **Paul y yo tenemos** trece años.
  c) **Vivimos** en una ciudad que se llama Pamplona.
  d) **Celebramos** su tercer cumpleaños ayer.

**Q3** a) ¿Cómo te llamas?
  b) ¿Eres del norte de España?
  c) ¿Cuándo es tu cumpleaños?
  d) ¿Dónde vives?

**Q4** Mi nombre es Yusef y tengo dieciséis años. Vivíamos en Madrid, pero ahora vivimos en Alicante. Mi hermano se llama Khaled. ¡Somos gemelos! Nuestro cumpleaños es el veintiocho de julio.

**Q5** My best friend is called Coral, but most of the time we call her Cori. Her date of birth is the 30th of March 2004, so her birthday falls the day after mine. Cori is of Peruvian nationality / is Peruvian.

### Page 8 — My Family

**Q1** a) Each / Every Friday, Zara and Dani go to the cinema with my stepsister.
  b) viven — I have some relatives who live in Wales.
  c) se llaman — Rita's cousins are called Jorge and Flora.
  d) tienen — My uncles / uncle and aunt / uncles and aunts have some adopted children.

**Q2** a) Mis hermanas mayores no viven con nosotros.
  b) daughters — El padrastro de Leah tiene tres hijas.
  c) nephews — ¿Conoces a mis sobrinos?
  d) brothers, sisters — Mi mujer no tiene hermanos / no tiene ni hermanos ni hermanas.

**Q3** a) hijo único / hija única
  b) preterite tense and present tense
  c) lo más importante / la cosa más importante
  Soy hijo único / hija única, pero paso mucho tiempo con mis primos/as. La semana pasada, mi tío se casó, así que mis primos/as tienen una madrastra. (Ella) se llama Lili y lo más importante / la cosa más importante es que es simpática.

**Q4** My grandparents like sitting in the park and listening to the children who are playing there / to sit in the park and listen to the children who play there. Yesterday they saw a man whose small children were greeting / saying hello to everyone in a very funny way. When I'm older, I would love to have children like them.

### Page 9 — Describing People

**Q1** a) Carlos tiene los ojos verdes.
  b) straight — José Luis tiene el pelo liso.
  c) slim — Nancy es bastante delgada.
  d) short, blonde — Tienen el pelo corto y rubio.
  e) black — Llevo gafas. Son negras.
  f) long, curly — Lisa y yo tenemos el pelo largo y rizado.

**Q2** a) Paula is taller than Erica.
  b) You are **much younger than** your cousin.
  c) I am **as good-looking as** Dan.
  d) Annabel **is not as strong as** my stepsister.

**Q3** a) Felipe used to have longer hair than me.
  b) llevaban — June and Neil used to wear plastic glasses.
  c) era — I used to be very short, but now I'm quite tall.
  d) quería — My sister always wanted a piercing.

**Q4** a) **Marisa:** Tenemos estas gafas azules. ¿Le gustan?
  **Nick:** Creo que son demasiado grandes. Tengo una cara bastante pequeña.
  b) **Marisa:** Si usted busca gafas más pequeñas, tenemos estas rojas.
  **Nick:** No, soy pelirrojo, así que preferiría tener otro color.
  c) **Marisa:** También vendemos gafas marrones. Muchos jóvenes llevan / Mucha gente joven lleva gafas como estas.
  **Nick:** ¡Me encantan! Gracias por su ayuda.

### Page 10 — Personalities

**Q1** a) Sometimes my cousin is understanding.
  b) Izzy is always lively and (she's) never lazy.
  c) From time to time, my younger brother is shy.
  d) My best friend is chatty and always funny.

**Q2** a) A good friend is generous.
  b) antipáticos — My enemies are very unpleasant.
  c) trabajadoras — Olivia and Carla seem hard-working.
  d) simpática — Your mum is usually friendly.

**Q3** a) No era valiente cuando era pequeño/a.
  b) Nerea y Ana nunca serán honestas / honradas. / Nerea y Ana no serán honestas / honradas nunca.
  c) No hay nadie tan perezoso/a como tú.
  d) Philip ya no es hablador.

**Q4** Hola Eva. (Yo) sé que a veces soy egoísta. Intentaré ser más generosa en el futuro y siempre compartiré mis caramelos contigo.
Lo siento mucho. Saskia.

# Answers

**Q5** My ideal boyfriend would be creative and active. A characteristic that I can't stand is arrogance. My ideal boyfriend would be someone who doesn't think that they're the most important person in the world. Moreover / Furthermore, I would like to go out with someone who has a good sense of humour and (who) makes me laugh.

## Page 11 — Pets

**Q1** **a)** Mi perro tiene los ojos <u>marrones</u>.
**b)** Tengo dos conejos <u>blancos</u>.
**c)** La tortuga de mis abuelos es muy <u>vieja</u>.
**d)** Normalmente, mi gato es <u>cariñoso</u>.
**e)** Mi amigo/a tiene <u>muchos</u> peces de colores.
**f)** Nuestros cobayos / conejillos de Indias son muy <u>graciosos</u>.

**Q2** **a)** conditional — I would like to have a grey cat.
**b)** imperfect — I used to have / I had two horses (who were) called Fred and Louis.
**c)** preterite — I went to an aquarium with my cousin and we saw tropical fish.
**d)** future — In the future, I will buy a big dog.
**e)** present — My friend has a guinea pig.
**f)** perfect — My sister's rabbit has eaten all (of) the lettuces in the garden.

**Q3** **a)** My little cat is very intelligent.
**b)** I have a **really small / tiny** dog (who is) called Iggie.
**c)** My hamster was / used to be **really fat**.
**d)** For me, it's **really important** to have a pet.

**Q4** Mi hermano quiere una mascota, así que voy a comprarle un conejo. El conejo tiene tres meses y es negro y blanco. Tiene la nariz rosa y orejas larguísimas. Es un animal muy bonito. Tendrá una casita en nuestro jardín.

## Page 12 — Style and Fashion

**Q1** **a)** Whose is this black cap?
**b)** Which (one) do you prefer, this blue blouse or that striped / stripy blouse?
**c)** Who did you buy this skirt with? / With whom did you buy this skirt?

**Q2** **a)** Me gusta tu pulsera / brazalete.
**b)** Les encanta mi corbata.
**c)** A Silvia le encantan las chaquetas de cuero / de piel.
**d)** A Dimitri le gustaría una camisa de algodón.

**Q3** **a)** Tania will buy a sweater instead of a t-shirt.
**b)** tendremos — Next year, we won't / will not have to wear uniform.
**c)** llevaré — If it's cold, I think I will wear a woollen scarf.
**d)** quedarán — Those trousers will suit you.

**Q4** Para mí, estar en la onda no es importante / no me importa. Es más importante elegir ropa cómoda. En el verano, me gusta llevar un pantalón corto en vez de vaqueros.

**Q5** Young people today / nowadays have very different styles. Some have an alternative style with tattoos while others have a more formal style. In my opinion, it's important to be fashionable and dress well. I think that everyone will wear clothes made from recycled materials when I'm older.

## Page 13 — Relationships

**Q1** **a)** I get on well with my younger sister.
**b)** Nos enamoramos — We fell in love a year ago.
**c)** me siento — I always feel relaxed with her.
**d)** Me divierto — I have fun / have a good time spending time with my friends.
**e)** relacionarme — I usually get on well with other people.
**f)** nos peleamos — Sometimes, my brother and I argue / fight.

**Q2** **a)** Mis hermanos y yo nos peleábamos mucho.
**b)** Tula y yo **teníamos** una buena relación.
**c)** Mi padre y yo **nos llevábamos** bien.
**d)** Mis primos siempre **me fastidiaban / molestaban / irritaban**.
**e)** No **conocía** a mi tío.

**Q3** Todos los lunes / Cada lunes visito a mi abuela. Nos llevamos muy bien y me apoya cuando tengo disputas / discusiones con mis amigos. No me juzgaría nunca, pero le fastidia mucho cuando hablo mientras estoy comiendo.

**Q4** **a)** **Miguel:** Do you get on well with your brothers / brothers and sisters, Tania?
**Tania:** When I was younger, no, but now I do.
**b)** **Adrián:** Do you know your nephew well, Mónica?
**Mónica:** No, unfortunately we don't know each other very well.
**c)** **Pilar:** How are things going with your boyfriend, Rosa?
**Rosa:** Everything's going well. I trust him and I think I've really fallen in love with him.

## Page 14 — Socialising with Friends and Family

**Q1** **a)** What are you going to do / What are you doing this weekend, Tamal?
**b)** I have a lot of relatives / relations who live near (to) me.
**c)** Raúl, do you have the present that we bought for Pedro?
**d)** I will go to a restaurant with my family, which will be fun.

**Q2** **a)** **Alana:** Me gusta pasar tiempo con mis hermanas cuando están de buen humor.
**b)** **Clara:** Lo odio cuando estoy estudiando y mi hermano está jugando con sus amigos.
**c)** **Maxi:** Es imposible hablar con mis padres cuando están cocinando.
**d)** **Resul:** Pues, (yo) prefiero salir con mis amigos. Si me quedo en casa, tengo que hacer de canguro.

# Answers

**e) Luna:** Mis primos/as son traviesos/as, así que no me gusta compartir mis cosas con ellos / ellas.

**Q3 a)** Yesterday I went to the theme park with my friends.

**b)** hablé — I didn't talk to Rafael because he was conceited and spoilt.

**c)** Vi — I saw the film once with my aunt and again with my friend.

**d)** enseñó — My father taught the children how to play tennis.

**e)** llamó — My friend called me because she wanted advice.

**Q4** Mi mejor amigo se llama Paco. Nuestra amistad es muy importante para mí y él es la persona más leal / fiel que conozco. Por ejemplo, cuando otra gente en nuestra pandilla me intimidó / acosó el año pasado, (él) me apoyó. Nos encanta viajar juntos, así que el año que viene / el año próximo, iremos a Portugal.

## Page 15 — Partnership

**Q1 a)** I hope to get married to a kind / nice man.

**b)** I would like to **fall in love** in the future.

**c)** I intend to **have** at least one child.

**d)** I want a big party to **celebrate** my wedding.

**Q2 a)** Mi tío se casó con su vecino/a.

**b)** Conoció a alguien hace unas semanas.

**c)** Mis abuelos se separaron recientemente.

**d)** Sus amigos/as se comprometieron el fin de semana.

**e)** No quiero casarme porque me gusta estar soltero/a.

**Q3 a) Violeta:** Diego, the day we met, I decided that I wanted to spend the rest of my life with you. You are the person I love most in the world, so I want us to get married. What do you think?

**b) Diego:** Really? It would be fantastic! We have always got on well with each other and we're a great team. I can't wait!

**Q4** Mis padres están casados desde hace quince años. Parece que tienen un matrimonio feliz porque se ríen cuando están juntos y casi nunca se pelean. Espero casarme un día, pero mi madre me ha aconsejado que termine mis estudios primero.

## Pages 16-18 — Mixed Practice

**Q1 a)** Thank you for inviting me to your wedding. I would love to attend.

**b)** I'm inviting you to my birthday party next Tuesday.

**c)** I'm sorry to hear that your parents have decided to separate.

**d)** Congratulations on your wedding. I wish you all the best on this special day.

**e)** Is it true that you want a divorce? You've always seemed happy together.

**Q2** Iratxe has always liked cats. She has recently adopted a small grey and white cat called Toby. He's very lively, but he's very clumsy! Last week, he broke some glasses in the dining room. The good thing is that Iratxe doesn't mind, because she loves Toby a lot.

**Q3** Me llamo Oscar. Cuando era pequeño, era un poco travieso, pero no era ni perezoso ni egoísta. Ahora pienso que soy bastante callado. Mi mejor amigo, Marco, es muy educado / cortés y es más serio que yo. El año que viene / El año próximo iremos a colegios / institutos diferentes.

**Q4 Padre:** ¿Qué quieres para tu cumpleaños?
**Hijo:** Me gustaría tener un perro. Lo pasearía todos los días y jugaría con él en el jardín.
**Padre:** Un perro es una gran responsabilidad. ¿Quién cuidaría de él cuando estás en el colegio? No podríamos dejarlo solo en casa durante todo el día.
**Hijo:** No sé. Quizás sería mejor tener un pez de colores.

**Q5 a)** No aguanto a la novia de mi hermano. Es muy glotona y maleducada.

**b)** Su mujer es de altura mediana. Tiene los ojos verdes.

**c)** Se comprometió con un hombre delgado que tiene el pelo largo y castaño.

**d)** El sobrino de Roberto es muy joven. Tendrá dos años el enero que viene / el enero próximo.

**e)** Mi hermanastra es muy habladora. ¡Nunca para / deja de hablar!

**f)** El/La primo/a de Mika estaba celoso/a de su relación con Danilo.

**Q6** My sister writes a fashion blog / a blog about fashion. She has a retro style and wears quite old-fashioned clothes. Yesterday she put on a holey leather jacket / a leather jacket with holes in it. When she's an adult, she would like to be a writer for a fashion magazine. Personally, I like wearing more modern clothes.

**Q7 a)** Leila es mi gemela. Tenía el pelo largo, pero ahora tiene el pelo corto / lo tiene corto. Su novio es generoso y simpático. Me llevo muy bien con él.

**b)** El hermano menor de mi padre es de altura mediana. Es calvo y lleva gafas. Tiene un perro negro que se llama Hugo, que suele comportarse bien / ser obediente.

**c)** La semana pasada, nuestros abuelos se ocuparon de nosotros. Discutimos mucho porque pensaron que no nos comportamos bien, y que éramos demasiado inmaduros.

**d)** Mi tía es muy comprensiva. Cuando tengo un problema, siempre me da buenos consejos. Confío mucho en ella.

# Answers

**Q8** Mi primo se llama Andrés y nació el veintitrés de abril, ¡el mismo día que yo! Cada año, celebramos nuestros cumpleaños juntos. Este año, Andrés quiere ir a la bolera con unos amigos, pero yo preferiría ir a un restaurante. Con suerte, podremos hacer las dos cosas.

**Q9** **Lola:** I'm an only child. I would like to have siblings / brothers and sisters, but my parents don't want to have more children. Do you have any siblings / brothers and sisters, Ibón?
**Ibón:** Yes, I have a brother. I look a lot like him, although he has longer hair than me. My parents want him to cut his hair, but he doesn't want to.
**Lola:** My brother doesn't care about fashion. What's your brother like?
**Ibón:** He's a very independent person. He never wears branded clothes either.

**Q10 a)** Mi novio ideal sería simpático e inteligente. Tendría el pelo moreno y los ojos azules. Nos interesarían las mismas cosas.
**b)** Pasaría mi cumpleaños ideal con mi familia. Hace unos años, fui al zoo / parque zoológico con mis sobrinas y lo pasamos fenomenal.
**c)** La mejor amiga de Rico se llama Sophia. Les encantan pasear en el parque y jugar juntos. Era muy tímida cuando la conocí, pero ahora es más habladora.

**Q11** Hello / Hi, my name is Snow White. My family life has always been difficult. My father died two years ago, leaving me with my stepmother. She's jealous of me, especially my black hair. I would like to improve the relationship between us, but she spends all her time in her bedroom talking to her extremely ugly reflection.

**Q12** Are you looking for someone to take care of / look after your guinea pig when you go on holiday? I started working with animals twelve years ago and I'm responsible and hard-working. I know that pets are members of the family, so I will care for / look after your guinea pig as if it were my own / mine. If you want more information, call me or send me an email.

## Section 3 — Technology, Free Time and Customs & Festivals

### Page 19 — Technology

**Q1** **a)** I will send a text message to Ángel.
**b)** present tense — We can look for a photo on the Internet.
**c)** imperfect tense — Flora used to do / was doing her homework on her laptop.
**d)** present tense, perfect tense — Are you sure that you've saved your work?

**Q2** **a)** ¿Te gusta mi móvil nuevo, Julia?
**b)** Your, his — Tu hermano quiere un ordenador para su cumpleaños.
**c)** Her — Su amigo recibe mucho correo basura.
**d)** Our — Nuestro/a profesor/a dice que la tecnología es una herramienta educativa fenomenal.

**Q3** **a)** You should never give others access to your personal files.
**b)** It's important to choose a secure password.
**c)** I used to use the Internet to access my bank account.
**d)** Nowadays, you must protect your identity online.
**e)** Paula always deletes her messages after reading them.

**Q4** In the past, people used to use letters and telephone calls to communicate. Nowadays, they prefer to use technology to send emails or text messages. I think there will be even more technology in the future. If I had to stop using my devices, I don't know what I'd do!

### Page 20 — Social Media

**Q1** **a)** Every day, my brother posts photos of himself on his blog.
**b)** pierde — Our father always loses his password.
**c)** Suelo — I usually chat to my classmates / school friends on social media.
**d)** me acuesto — At night, I go to bed late because I'm surfing the Internet.
**e)** quiere — My mother wants to learn to use social media.

**Q2** **a)** A veces uso las salas de chat / los chats para hablar con mis primos en Australia.
**b)** **Ayer**, Elena decidió desactivar su cuenta.
**c)** Cuando mi amiga tiene un problema, pide consejo en las redes sociales **a menudo**.
**d)** **Generalmente**, no uso las salas de chat / los chats porque pueden ser peligrosas/os.

**Q3** **a)** The good thing about social networks is that you can contact your friends at any time.
**b)** It's possible to be addicted to social media. My friend / a friend of mine had / used to have problems with her studies due to her addiction.

**Q4** Una desventaja de los medios sociales es que puedes / se puede ser víctima del acoso cibernético. Tuve que bloquear a personas que escribieron cosas desagradables sobre lo que había colgado. Me preocupa todavía entonces no uso las redes sociales con mucha frecuencia / a menudo. Pienso que es muy importante estar seguro en línea / en la red.

### Page 21 — Music

**Q1** **a)** Last week, I played the guitar with my stepdad.
**b)** escucharon — Víctor and Gorka listened to rock music in the morning.
**c)** aprendió — Catarina learnt the lyrics of her favourite songs.
**d)** fue — My sister went to a concert with her girlfriend.

**Q2** **a)** El mes pasado, fui a un concierto con mis tíos / mi tía y mi tío.
**b)** Descarga música en vez de comprar CDs.
**c)** Su profesor/a de música toca la batería en un grupo / una banda.

# Answers

**Q3** listening to the radio; that song; I fell in love with their music; I can't stop listening to it

**Q4** Cuando era más joven, tocaba la flauta. Fui miembro/a de una orquesta durante tres años. Recientemente decidí aprender a tocar otro instrumento. Toco el piano desde hace seis meses y me encanta. Me gustaría escribir mis propias canciones en el futuro.

## Page 22 — Cinema and TV

**Q1** a) The film we saw had a fantastic plot.
  b) principal**es** — The lead / main actors won a prize for their roles.
  c) policíac**as** — I hate police shows because there's too much violence.
  d) preferid**o** — My favourite programme is about a boy called Félix.

**Q2** a) **Jimena**: A mí me gustan mucho los dibujos animados porque me hacen reír.
  **Lucas**: A mí también, pero me importan más las noticias. Me interesa saber lo que está pasando en el mundo.
  b) **Thiago**: ¿Es verdad que te fastidian / te molestan las telenovelas, Maite?
  **Maite**: Sí, no me gustan para nada. No entiendo por qué las ves, Thiago.

**Q3** a) El viernes vi la televisión durante más de tres horas.
  b) Íbamos al cine **los domingos** porque era más barato.
  c) Alejandro va a ver una película de ciencia ficción **el miércoles**.
  d) Veo mi programa preferido **los martes**.

**Q4** I usually watch TV with my mum and my sister in the evening. We like different programmes, so we don't always agree on what to watch. My sister used to hate reality shows, but now she really enjoys / likes them. My mum prefers to watch quiz shows because she loves to answer all the questions.

## Page 23 — Hobbies and Role Models

**Q1** a) Ellos / Ellas hicieron excursionismo en Escocia, pero nosotros hicimos submarinismo en Portugal.
  b) Yo suelo leer cuentos de espías / de espionaje, pero ella prefiere leer novelas de fantasía.
  c) Tú juegas al ajedrez en tu tiempo libre, pero él juega a la petanca.

**Q2** a) I've already read that comic, so I'm going to buy another (one).
  b) aquellas — I would like to go horse riding in those mountains (over there).
  c) este — This author's new book is / comes out soon.
  d) Esa — That athlete is a role model for children.

**Q3** a) conditional and present
  b) compete
  c) for

I would like to be an athlete. There are lots of people who inspire me, especially athletes who compete in the Olympic Games. I admire them because they train for four years to represent their country. They should be proud of what they achieve.

**Q4** Mi hermanastra ha escrito cinco libros para niños. Escribía cuentos cortos cuando (yo) era pequeño/a. La admiro porque es muy imaginativa y creativa. Cuando sea mayor, me gustaría ser escritor/a también. Sin embargo, preferiría escribir cuentos / novelas de aventura o de misterio para adultos.

## Page 24 — Food

**Q1** a) Él probó muchos de los platos en la mesa.
  b) Hay pocas frutas más ricas / sabrosas que los melocotones.
  c) Sus padres no creen / piensan que yo coma bastantes verduras.
  d) Esas son algunas de las salchichas más saladas que nunca he probado.

**Q2** a) My boyfriend went out to buy drinks while I prepared the food.
  b) cuando — Everything was ready when our friends arrived for the party.
  c) así que — My brother doesn't know how to cook so he eats a lot of fast food.
  d) porque — I go to cooking classes because I want to learn to prepare tasty / delicious food.

**Q3** a) Añade el azúcar a la crema / nata.
  b) No **hiervas** la col.
  c) Después de cocinar la carne, **corta** las patatas.
  d) **Cocina** el arroz antes de preparar la salsa.

**Q4** My neighbour is vegetarian. He always makes the most of the fruits and vegetables that he grows in his greenhouse. Last week, he invited me to lunch. He cooked a plate / dish of peppers, carrots and peas with a spicy sauce. I liked it so much that I asked him for the recipe. I hope I can prepare it as well as him / he did!

## Page 25 — Eating Out

**Q1** a) What drink do you recommend? I'm very thirsty.
  b) prefiere — What type / kind of food do you prefer when you're hungry?
  c) puede — Can you give us a discount?
  d) trae — Can you bring us the bill please? Is the tip included?

**Q2** a) Mi restaurante preferido está en el centro de la ciudad.
  b) Las chuletas de cerdo con salsa de nata / crema **son** deliciosas.
  c) Los camareros **están** muy amables hoy.
  d) El cocinero / la cocinera **está** preparando nuestra comida.
  e) Mi postre preferido **es** la tarta de manzana.

# Answers

**Q3 a) Agustín:** ¿Todavía quieres compartir un primer plato, Bianca?
**Bianca:** Sí, me apetece pedir las gambas de nuevo / otra vez.
**b) Agustín:** Deberíamos / debemos pedir las bebidas en seguida / enseguida.
**Bianca:** Buena idea, me gustaría probar el vino blanco.
**c) Agustín:** Tengo mucha hambre. Espero que nuestra comida llegue pronto.
**Bianca:** Yo también. Voy a tomar postre después.

**Q4** Did I tell you (about) what happened at the restaurant yesterday? The waiter forgot what I had ordered and (he) brought me some pork chops instead of the squid. When it arrived at / got to the table, the food was cold, so I complained to the boss. When I spoke to / with him, he was very rude and didn't give me a discount. Therefore / So I didn't give him a tip.

## Pages 26-27 — Sport

**Q1 a)** I ride my bike / cycle to school daily / every day because it's quicker than taking / catching the bus.
**b)** pocas veces, siempre — Andrea rarely goes skating because she's always busy.
**c)** de vez en cuando — We go mountain climbing from time to time, when the weather permits / allows (us).
**d)** Normalmente — Normally, they go to the sports field on Sunday mornings.

**Q2 a)** Usualmente / Normalmente, hago piragüismo con mi hermana menor.
**b)** Jugar al fútbol es **mejor** cuando hace buen tiempo.
**c)** La equitación / Montar a caballo es **el peor** deporte cuando llueve.
**d)** Mi hermano es **el mejor** nadador de nuestra familia.

**Q3** twice a week; the athletics track; canoeing; ice rink; go there to skate.

**Q4 a)** was — Jugaba al fútbol cuando era más joven pero ahora juego al tenis.
**b)** (used to) love — A Veronica le encantaba jugar al hockey e ir de pesca / ir a pescar.
**c)** were playing — Cuando llegué al polideportivo, jugaban al baloncesto / estaban jugando al baloncesto.
**d)** were — Estábamos cerca del estadio cuando perdimos el balón / la pelota.

**Q5 a)** I love swimming. I go to the swimming pool with my friends almost every day.
**b)** del — Miguel used to be a fan of / fanatical about cycling but now he prefers badminton.
**c)** al —We often go to school on Saturdays to play netball.
**d)** al, en — We went to the park this weekend on skateboards.

**Q6 a) Chami:** Me gusta jugar al tenis con mis amigos en el verano.
**b) Raúl:** Hacer deportes es una buena manera de pasar tiempo juntos y divertirnos.
**c) Sami:** Siempre veo los Juegos Olímpicos de Invierno porque mi deporte preferido es el esquí.
**d) Clara:** En el futuro, me encantaría ir a ver un partido de fútbol en persona.
**e) Juan:** Hago equitación / Monto a caballo desde hace siete años.

**Q7** Mi abuelo es muy deportista. Practica la vela casi todos los días y a menudo juega al voleibol en la playa. Cuando era más joven, hacía / practicaba muchos deportes de riesgo pero tuvo que dejar de hacerlos / practicarlos porque se rompió la pierna. Intenta / Está intentando enseñarme a practicar la vela pero pienso / creo / opino que es demasiado difícil.

**Q8** I've always loved rugby. In my opinion, it is the best sport in the world. I'm looking forward to going to see a match. Next week a rugby tournament will be taking place / take place at the stadium. I'm very lucky because my parents bought tickets so that we would be able to see / watch it.

## Pages 28-29 — Customs and Festivals

**Q1 a)** A tu hermana le encanta la feria.
**b)** Their — Sus padres bailaron a la fiesta.
**c)** my — La Navidad es un día festivo en mi país.
**d)** our — Las fiestas durante la Pascua son nuestra tradición.

**Q2 a)** Las Fallas es una fiesta valenciana / de Valencia que empieza el quince de marzo.
**b)** El seis de enero muchos españoles celebran el Día de Reyes.
**c)** Las celebraciones del Día de los Muertos empiezan a medianoche el primero de noviembre.

**Q3 a)** This year my parents are going to Pamplona, where there is a festival in which people run down / through the streets followed by bulls.
**b)** I hate bullfights because they're very cruel. My brother thinks that they're an art form / a form of art, which really angers me / makes me very angry.
**c)** A friend of mine has an uncle who was a bullfighter / matador. Bullfighting is a tradition of which he's very proud / which he's very proud of.

**Q4** El veinte de enero; celebran; se disfraza de; El festival / La fiesta empieza; durante veinticuatro horas sin parar.

**Q5 a)** ¿Adónde fuiste la Navidad pasada?
**b)** ¿Cómo celebras el Día de Reyes?
**c)** ¿Qué haces la Nochebuena?
**d)** ¿Cuándo es la Pascua este año?

# Answers

**Q6**  **a)** human towers
**b)** on top of
**c)** constructing / building them
Castells is one of the most important cultural traditions in Catalonia. People gather in the streets and build human towers by standing on top of each other / one on top of the other. It's amazing to watch / see them, but it can be very dangerous for the people who take part in constructing / building them.

**Q7**  **a)** celebrate, saw, took part.
Mi prima fue a Colombia para celebrar el Carnaval de Barranquilla. Vio la Gran Parada y participó en la Batalla de Flores.
**b)** travel, visit, participate.
El año que viene / El año próximo, mi madre y yo viajaremos a Buñol. Visitaremos a mis tíos, quienes participan en la Tomatina cada año / todos los años.
**c)** go, seeing, watch, try, enjoy.
Si vas a Bilbao en agosto, vale la pena ver las celebraciones de Aste Nagusia. Mira los desfiles, prueba la comida y disfruta el día.

**Q8**  This summer, I went to Jávea. I took part / participated in a festival that remembers / to remember the battle / fight between two different cultures to rule the land. There were lots of colourful parades, music concerts and fireworks. I learnt a lot about the history of the area and I'd like to go back and celebrate it in the future.

## Pages 30-32 — Mixed Practice

**Q1**  **a)** A menudo Bruno utiliza / usa las redes sociales para compartir la música de su grupo / banda.
**b)** Era más barato comprar las entradas para el concierto en Internet / en línea.
**c)** He visto muchos anuncios en los medios sociales para una nueva comedia.
**d)** Quería ver el programa en Internet pero ya no está disponible.

**Q2**  **a)** Hernando was given an e-reader for his birthday, but he doesn't use it. He's always preferred paper books.
**b)** Renata loves to read. I never see her without a newspaper in her hand. Her parents would prefer that she did more sport but she doesn't like it.
**c)** I have lots of hobbies. On Wednesdays I usually do martial arts. At weekends / At the weekend, I like to play board games with my friends.

**Q3**  **a)** Álvaro se graba cuando toca la trompeta y cuelga los vídeos en Internet / en la red.
**b)** Tocar el clarinete era una de sus aficiones preferidas.
**c)** Vimos un documental sobre el uso de las castañuelas en la música tradicional de España / la música española tradicional.

**d)** A mi madre le encanta la música de ópera. A menudo la escucha en su portátil.
**e)** Sigo a mi música preferida en las redes sociales para escuchar sus canciones nuevas.

**Q4**  Mi madre piensa que soy perezoso/a porque siempre navego por Internet / la red. Cuando era pequeño/a, jugaba al baloncesto fuera con mis amigos. Ahora prefiero quedarme en casa y jugar a los videojuegos. A menudo tenemos disputas sobre cuánto tiempo paso delante del ordenador.

**Q5**  Last year, my friend and I visited an isolated / a remote village where there is a festival that celebrates / to celebrate the grape harvest. It's a very famous event so there were lots of TV cameras that were recording all the action. Some journalists interviewed us / We were interviewed by some journalists and we saw ourselves on the news that day / that same day!

**Q6**  **Gael:** ¿Vienes al cine? Vamos a ver la nueva película de ciencia ficción.
**Isaías:** Dije que prepararía la cena para mi familia esta noche. ¿A qué hora vas / vais a ir?
**Gael:** Nos encontramos fuera del cine a las siete pero la película no empieza hasta las siete y media.
**Isaías:** Te enviaré / mandaré un mensaje (de texto) si puedo venir pero dudo que pueda.

**Q7**  **a)** Nerea decided to go to the festival after seeing the photos of the processions that her friend had posted on social media / networks.
**b)** My favourite video games are those in which you can do / play sport. I have some that use virtual reality.
**c)** Cooking has been his passion for eleven years. He is always looking for new recipes on the internet. When he is older, he wants to have his own pastry shop / cake shop.

**Q8**  **The Devil's Gloves**
I saw this great horror film on Thursday. It's based on a really popular TV show of the same name. It has lots of action and a thrilling / an exciting soundtrack. It's about a man who finds some gloves created / made by the devil. I'd recommend it to all my friends.

**Q9**  **a)** I prefer to watch / watching rugby tournaments in person than on the TV. There is a better atmosphere in the stadium than in my living room.
**b)** Watching sport online has become very popular because it is very convenient. You can watch matches and tournaments without leaving the house.
**c)** As a footballer, I want fans to come to the stadium to watch matches. It is much more exciting than watching them on their computers.

# Answers

**Q10** Stitchton Café es el lugar perfecto para relajarse después de jugar al deporte / hacer deporte en la playa. Nuestros balcones ofrecen buenas vistas / una gran vista de las canchas de voleibol. Cada sábado en junio, habrá música y baile a partir de las ocho de la tarde / noche. Para empezar / comenzar, después del torneo de voleibol esta semana, tenemos / vamos a dar una fiesta en la playa.

**Q11 a) Iker:** Did you go to the food festival on Saturday? There were so many dishes and I loved them all.
**b) Nina:** Of course! I went with my parents. We tried some veal steaks cooked with garlic and ground pepper.
**c) Iker:** How delicious! Did you see the competition in the afternoon?
**d) Nina:** No, we didn't see it. Which (dish) won? If I had to choose my favourite dish, it would be the chicken and prawn paella.

**Q12** El ídolo de Fabiana acaba de abrir un nuevo restaurante en el centro de la ciudad. Ha visto los programas de cocina en la televisión desde (que era) pequeña entonces le encantaría probar sus platos. El único problema es que no ha podido reservar una mesa todavía porque el restaurante es muy popular.

## Section 4 — Where You Live

## Page 33 — Where You Live

**Q1 a)** When he was younger, he lived in the countryside.
**b)** iban — The boys / children were going / went / used to go to school.
**c)** tenía — I had to walk to the supermarket.
**d)** visitábamos — We used to visit / visited the flower market.

**Q2** Sentences **a)**, **c)** and **d)** should be ticked.
**a)** La ciudad tiene una población bastante pequeña.
**b)** El ayuntamiento se encuentra / está en la zona peatonal.
**c)** Hay una mezquita preciosa en el centro de la ciudad.
**d)** Me gusta ir a la pastelería en nuestro pueblo.

**Q3 a)** she has just moved.
**b)** north-west.
**c)** pluperfect.
Carmen has just moved to Santiago de Compostela, a city in the north-west of Spain. She likes the city because it is very lively and it has a magnificent church. Last year, she lived in Barcelona because she had always wanted to live near the sea.

**Q4** Me gusta vivir en una ciudad porque es divertido y siempre hay algo que hacer. Hace dos años, un restaurante grande y una sala de fiestas moderna abrieron sus puertas cerca del puerto. No me gustaría vivir en el campo porque no hay muchas tiendas y es aburrido allí.

## Page 34 — The Home

**Q1** boarding house; outskirts; I feel isolated; flat; town / city centre; move house.

**Q2 a)** My family's house is very small.
**b)** está — The lounge / living room is opposite the kitchen.
**c)** están — Both bathrooms are on the second floor.
**d)** son — The stairs in our house are narrow.

**Q3 a)** El cuadro cuelga en la pared.
**b)** Hay un río pequeño **al lado de su casa**.
**c)** La granja está situada **en las montañas**.
**d)** Se mudan **a un nuevo piso**.

**Q4** Me mudé de casa cuando cumplí dieciocho años. No me gustaba compartir una habitación con mi hermana. En mi piso, mi cuarto preferido es la cocina porque es grande y hay sillas cómodas en la mesa de comedor. Desafortunadamente, mi dormitorio es pequeñito y no tiene ventana.

## Page 35 — Home Life

**Q1 a)** temprano — Each day, I wake up early to take the dog for a walk.
**b)** De vez en cuando — From time to time, I have cereal without much milk / with not a lot of milk.
**c)** todos los días, nunca — Every day, I shower before I go to bed and I never forget.
**d)** a menudo, casi nunca — I often have lunch at school and I almost never go out to eat.

**Q2 a)** Me levanto temprano pero siempre estoy cansado/a.
**b)** Robert **se despierta** tarde los fines de semana.
**c)** Laura siempre **se sienta** cuando vuelve a casa.
**d)** Mis padres **se visten** mientras escuchan la radio.

**Q3 a) Samara:** Mi madre siempre me despierta a las siete para el desayuno.
**Carlos:** Me levanto a las seis y media (de la mañana) para ducharme antes de desayunar.
**b) Samara:** ¿Haces la cama antes de ducharte o después?
**Carlos:** Me olvido de hacerla a menudo porque no estoy muy organizado por la mañana.
**c) Samara:** Usualmente, hago / Suelo hacer las tareas domésticas después del colegio. Ayer, corté el césped.
**Carlos:** Tuve que sacar la basura anoche. ¡Fue asqueroso! / ¡Qué asco!

**Q4** I think that getting up early is the best way to start the day. You can exercise, walk the dog, shower and prepare breakfast for everyone before they wake up. The children never go to bed when I ask them to, so it's difficult to get them up in the morning.

## Pages 36-37 — Shopping

**Q1 a)** I'm looking for a white cotton shirt.
**b)** negro<u>s</u> — I would like to buy a pair of black trousers.

# Answers

c) ro**ja**, amaril**lo** — I want a red scarf to wear with my yellow coat.

d) azul**es** — I would like to buy some blue earrings.

**Q2** a) Quisiera cien gramos de este queso.

b) Necesito una docena de **esos** huevos, por favor.

c) Quisiera un paquete de **estas** uvas y la mitad de **ese** jamón.

d) Deme medio kilo de **aquellas** zanahorias.

**Q3** a) una — He wants a jar of jam and a box of chocolate biscuits.

b) un, unas — I need a kilo of onions and some tins of tomatoes.

c) unas, una — She needs some bottles of olive oil and a loaf of bread.

d) un, unos — Give me a piece of this fruit pie, and some slices of that cake.

**Q4** a) Esta tienda solo tiene unas pocas tallas diferentes.

b) ¿Tienes bastante dinero para comprar toda esta ropa?

c) Había tanta gente en los grandes almacenes el sábado.

d) Voy a la misma tienda para comprar la ropa porque tiene muchos estilos.

e) Compré demasiados vestidos en las rebajas y necesito devolverlos.

**Q5** a) Mañana, voy a devolver esta falda.

b) Mi hermana **va a pedir** un reembolso al cajero / a la cajera.

c) Creo que **van a quejarse** al jefe.

d) **Vamos a cambiar** estos vestidos por esos / aquellos.

**Q6** a) Give me another carton of grape juice; a full one this time.

b) I want a cheese sandwich with lettuce and several packets of crisps.

c) The recipe is very complicated. We're missing half of what we need.

d) In the supermarket, you have to weigh vegetables before you take them / taking them to the till.

e) Juan and Carla need to go shopping more often because their fridge is always empty.

f) Your stepsister needed to buy all the ingredients before starting to cook.

**Q7** I used to go to the town centre to buy food but now I do it online. It's very convenient since you can do it at any time of day and you don't have to leave the house. However, it's easy to spend money without thinking about it. I still prefer going to the shops to buy clothes.

**Q8** **Blanca:** Quisiera cambiar este chándal azul, por favor.
**David:** ¿Hay algún problema?
**Blanca:** Las mangas son demasiadas cortas. También, el cierre de los pantalones está roto.
**David:** Le traeré otro. ¿Qué talla necesita?
**Blanca:** Talla 40, por favor.
**David:** Aquí lo tiene. Le he dado un descuento.

## Page 38 — Directions

**Q1** a) Tome / Toma la quinta calle después de los semáforos.

b) Está después del segundo puente.

c) Siga / Sigue la cuarta calle hasta el final.

d) Es el tercer edificio a la izquierda.

**Q2** a) The car park is behind the library.

b) al lado de — The sports / leisure centre is over there, next to the church.

c) enfrente de — The hairdresser's is opposite the butcher's.

d) entre — The bookshop is between the tobacconist's and the bakery.

e) delante del — The police station is in front of the town hall.

**Q3** doble; Pase; siga; doble; siga; Cruce.

**Q4** To get to the farm, it's better to go by car because / since it's a bit isolated. Go past the station and turn right when you see the second set of traffic lights. Then, cross the bridge and go straight on. It will be about 500 metres from there, at the end of the street.

## Page 39 — Weather

**Q1** a) In central Spain, it was very windy.

b) Hizo — It was cold in the north of England.

c) estuvo — In north-west France, it was hot.

d) hubo — On Friday, there were showers in the south.

**Q2** a) Hace mucho calor allá.

b) everywhere — Está nublado y hace frío por / en todas partes.

c) here, there — Aquí está lloviendo pero ahí solamente hace viento.

d) nearby — Hay tormentas con truenos y relámpagos cerca.

**Q3** a) imperfect subjunctive

b) either / neither / nor

c) lightning

I love it when it's sunny because you can go to the beach. It would be ideal / perfect if it was never humid because I don't sleep well at night. I don't feel well when it's very dry either. When it's stormy, I like to see / watch the lightning.

**Q4** La temperatura aquí en Gran Bretaña es muy diferente de España. El día en que visitamos Londres, no hizo mal tiempo por la mañana pero empezó a llover por la tarde. De momento / Actualmente estamos en Gales donde hace viento y hace frío. Mañana viajaremos a Escocia. ¡Espero que haga sol y haga calor ahí!

# Answers

## Pages 40-42 — Mixed Practice

**Q1** **a) Rosa:** El pronóstico para el fin de semana es bueno, así que quiero comprar este vestido.
**María:** Me encanta el color pero es demasiado grande. Te traeré uno más pequeño.

**b) Juan:** ¿Puedo pedir prestada tu chaqueta azul esta noche? No quiero tener frío en la fiesta.
**Diego**: Por supuesto, está en la silla al lado de la puerta.

**c) Pilar:** Hace tanto viento que se ha roto mi paraguas. ¿Puedo comprar otro por aquí?
**Sofía:** Sí y hay un descuento si compra dos (a la vez).

**Q2** Guillermo used to live in the mountains. He loved to play rugby there, but it was often stormy. When the team couldn't play outside, they / he went to the sports centre on the outskirts of town. Now he plays for a team in a nearby city and hopes that rugby can be his career.

**Q3** **a)** Mis abuelos viven en el campo. Era un lugar tranquilo pero una empresa local construyó una fábrica cerca. Ahora hay mucho ruido y humo.

**b)** Mis padres van a mudarse de casa cuando mis hermanas menores (se) vayan a la universidad porque su casa será demasiado grande para ellos.

**c)** Desafortunadamente la calefacción no funciona en mi nuevo piso así que tendré que llamar a un ingeniero para repararla. Sin embargo, me gusta mucho el piso porque tiene luz y es espacioso.

**Q4** Yesterday, we went to the coast because it was very sunny. We swam in the sea and afterwards we spent the rest of the day sitting on the beach until it started to get cold. I wanted to go shopping this morning because I'm going to a party next week. Unfortunately my mum couldn't take me to the shopping centre.

**Q5** **a)** A mí no me gusta mi barrio porque siempre está demasiado concurrido y la circulación / el tráfico es terrible.

**b)** Me gustaría vivir en otro sitio. Preferiría vivir en el campo donde es más tranquilo.

**c)** Esta mañana, fui a la librería por mis padres y acabo de volver.

**d)** Mi hermana hace la compra de la comida / la compra de comestibles y mi hermano limpia la cocina.

**e)** La semana pasada, empecé a trabajar en la carnicería pero todavía no sé mucho de carne.

**f)** La semana que viene / la próxima semana, aprenderé como cortar y pesar la carne para los clientes.

**Q6** In our old house, the lounge / living room was opposite the kitchen and there was a small bathroom on the left-hand side of the stairs. In our current house, the kitchen is at the end of the first floor corridor / corridor on the first floor. When we redecorate the house, we'll have to keep / store the furniture in the basement so that it doesn't get damaged.

**Q7** **a) Laura:** Are you coming for lunch next Thursday?
**Nico:** Yes, I can't wait. You live near the port don't you?

**b) Laura:** Yes, go past the museum that's next to the police station and follow that road / street to the end.
**Nico:** What is your house like?

**c) Laura:** It's the third semi-detached house on the right-hand side of the road / street.
**Nico:** Perfect. I'll call you if I can't find it.

**Q8** **a)** El mejor sitio para aparcar cuando llueve / está lloviendo es el aparcamiento al lado del ayuntamiento.

**b)** Habrá hielo este fin de semana. Voy a coger el autobús al centro de la ciudad en vez de conducir porque es / está más seguro.

**c)** La tormenta de ayer dañó varios barcos en el puerto.

**d)** Nevaba mucho en el invierno. Las fábricas de la ciudad tenían que cerrarse a menudo porque los trabajadores no podían llegar.

**Q9** **a) Juan:** ¿Quieres ir de compras mañana? Tengo que devolver unos zapatos.
**Emilia:** Sí, vendré contigo. Quisiera comprar un bañador nuevo.

**b) Juan:** Si no llueve, nos encontramos en el parque delante de la estación de autobuses a las diez.
**Emilia:** Bien, pero si hace mal tiempo, vamos a la cafetería adonde fuimos el mes pasado.

**c) Juan:** No me acuerdo dónde está. ¿Está cerca de la comisaría?
**Emilia:** Está al final de la calle mayor, al lado del museo a la izquierda / a mano izquierda.

**Q10** When I go shopping, I like to walk into the centre instead of driving. However, coming back with full bags is difficult when it's as hot as it is today. Tomorrow, I have lots of things to buy / to buy lots of things and I hope that it's less humid than today. I couldn't go yesterday because I hadn't been paid my wages.

**Q11** **a)** La semana pasada, me levanté a las seis y media, paseé al perro y me vestí para ir al instituto. Sin embargo, el instituto tuvo que cerrarse a causa de la nieve.

**b)** El jueves, estaba lavando mi coche cuando vi a mi vecino. Estaba saliendo de la casa con su mujer para dar un paseo.

**c)** Voy a limpiar mi piso más tarde. El viernes vienen a cenar unos amigos y no tendré tiempo para hacerlo antes de que lleguen.

# Answers

**Q12** In two weeks, it will be my uncle's birthday. I always used to buy him a cake from the same bakery. However, it closed down last month so I'll have to make him one myself. I think I'll need half a kilo of flour, half a dozen eggs, a packet of sugar and some butter.

## Section 5 — Lifestyle and Social & Global Issues

### Page 43 — Healthy Living

**Q1** a) In the morning, we went to the pool together.
b) bebió — She drank a lot of water after her boxing class.
c) dormí — Last night, I slept for more than nine hours.
d) jugué — Yesterday I played badminton with my friends.

**Q2** a) You must / should eat well (in order) to have enough energy.
b) por — People usually exercise for one or two hours at a time.
c) por — She runs through the streets every Saturday to the sports centre.
d) Para — To keep fit, athletes have to follow a healthy lifestyle / lead a healthy life.

**Q3** Doing; keep; Leading; eat; Avoiding; try; eat; drink; sleep.
Hacer ejercicio cada semana le ayudará a mantenerse en forma. Llevar una vida saludable significa que se debe comer una dieta equilibrada. Evitar la comida basura es importante y se debe intentar comer sano. También es importante beber mucha agua y dormir bastante.

**Q4** In general, I think I lead a healthy life / have a healthy lifestyle. I try to eat well and exercise regularly / often. I should eat more fruit but I don't really like it. Instead, I try to eat lots of vegetables. When I was young, my parents never gave me fish, but now I eat it several times a week.

### Page 44 — Unhealthy Living

**Q1** a) No me gusta el olor del humo.
b) Ninguno/a de mis amigos/as toma drogas.
c) No querría nunca / jamás hacer daño / dañar a los pulmones.
d) No conozco a nadie que bebe el alcohol.
e) Ni mi madre ni mi padre nunca / jamás ha fumado.
f) Mi tía ya no come comida basura.

**Q2** a) My uncle drank / used to drink juice instead of drinking alcohol.
b) You should do something to relax **before going to bed**.
c) **After smelling** the cigarette smoke, I felt ill.
d) We would prefer to go dancing **instead of getting drunk**.

**Q3** a) **Ruiz:** Mi padre dejó de fumar el año pasado. Fue muy difícil.
**Juan:** Mi madre fuma todavía pero yo quiero que lo deje.
b) **Rosa:** Cuando salgo (afuera) durante el verano, siempre llevo un sombrero.
**Gabi:** Yo también. Es importante protegerse del sol.
c) **Samara:** No querría tomar drogas. Es muy difícil parar / dejarlas.
**Jaime:** Sí, y a menudo, la gente tiene síndrome de abstinencia malo.

**Q4** At my school, there are some young people who take drugs. The problem has got worse recently and it could be because of peer pressure. I don't ever / never want to take drugs. Those who take drugs find it difficult to concentrate on their studies. They always feel tired and they could develop health problems / problems with their health in the future.

### Page 45 — Illnesses

**Q1** a) le duele — My sister's throat hurts.
b) nos duelen — Our legs hurt.
c) me duelen — My knees hurt.
d) le duele — Her head hurts.

**Q2** a) Él tendrá que ir al hospital porque se ha roto la pierna.
b) we'll take — Ella se despertó con dolor de oídos, así que la llevaremos a un doctor / médico.
c) won't get better — El problema de la obesidad juvenil no mejorará sin la intervención del gobierno.
d) he will need — Si su ataque de pánico no desaparece, él necesitará una ambulancia.
e) it will be — El año que viene / el año próximo, será obligatorio vacunar a los niños.

**Q3** a) **Jacob:** My mum wanted me to ask you if you have (any) allergies.
**Mateo:** I had a reaction to nuts two years ago but never since then.
b) **María:** When I breathe, I feel like I don't get enough air in my lungs.
**Alexa:** Do you have asthma? You should make an appointment with a doctor.
c) **Remi:** My brother fell (over) on Monday and broke his arm.
**Luis:** What a pity / shame! I broke my arm last year and had to have surgery.

**Q4** Hace unos meses, me encontré / estuve muy enfermo/a pero me siento mejor ahora. Perdí mucho peso y me sentí cansado/a todo el tiempo. El médico dice que estoy estresado/a. Necesitaré tomarme tiempo libre del trabajo para poder mejorarme. Espero sentirme mejor pronto.

### Pages 46-47 — Environmental Problems

**Q1** a) La gente tira demasiada basura y no creo que sea necesario.

**b)** Hay tantas cosas simples que podemos hacer para ayudar al medio ambiente.

**c)** No reciclamos bastante plástico, y esto daña el medio ambiente.

**d)** Poca gente se da cuenta de la severidad del problema del cambio climático.

**Q2 a)** We will turn off our electricals / electrical devices.

**b)** vería — I dreamt / used to dream that I wouldn't see rubbish on the beaches any more.

**c)** actuará — The government will act when it sees the damage.

**d)** andarían — If they had time, they would walk instead of driving.

**e)** sabréis — You will (all) soon know the effects of waste.

**Q3 a)** It is important that we look after our planet.

**b)** reciclemos — It is terrible that we don't recycle enough.

**c)** cortemos — It is sad that we cut down so many trees in the Amazon rainforest.

**d)** hagamos — It is essential that we do something to reduce the use of plastic / plastic use.

**e)** usemos — It is crucial that we use more renewable energy.

**Q4 a)** Debemos apagar las luces para que podamos ahorrar energía.

**b)** El cambio climático me preocupa porque no se está mejorando.

**c)** El plástico puede ser peligroso para las criaturas marinas / del mar si la gente lo tira en el mar.

**d)** Las compañías deben ayudar a desarrollar la energía renovable y maneras nuevas de utilizarla.

**Q5 a)** Al principio, la gente no creía en el calentamiento global.

**b) Aprendimos** mucho sobre la energía solar en nuestra clase ayer.

**c) Sabíamos** muy poco de la capa de ozono.

**d)** La semana pasada, el gobierno **decidió** bajar los niveles de polución / contaminación.

**Q6** I think the government should do more to reduce pollution. I live in Lima and there is so much traffic which produces environmental and noise pollution. It is essential that we teach children about the serious damage (that) pollution causes.

**Q7 a) Pedro:** We must combat the problem of deforestation.

**b) Raquel:** We have to do something because the rainforest / jungle is disappearing quickly / rapidly.

**c) Luisa:** I don't think it's just the government's responsibility.

**d) Dante:** In my opinion, the most serious problem is river contamination / the contamination / pollution of the rivers.

**e) Enzo:** People blame the greenhouse effect for environmental problems.

**Q8** Los desastres naturales siempre han sido un problema pero son más frecuentes ahora que antes. Hay inundaciones, huracanes y sequías en las noticias cada semana. Las acciones de todo el mundo / todos contribuye(n) al cambio climático y la situación es muy grave / seria. Debemos hacer algo para proteger la Tierra y evitar más daño.

## Page 48 — Problems in Society

**Q1 a)** The optimists still thought that there wouldn't be a war / the war wouldn't happen.

**b)** vivían — The most needy (people) lived in temporary accommodation.

**c)** veíamos — We saw the violence first hand.

**d)** era — Injustice was worse than the year before / the previous year.

**Q2 a)** Racism and inequality have no place in today's / contemporary society.

**b)** We could build homes for (the) people who need them.

**c)** I think the government should do more to help homeless people / the homeless.

**d)** War destroys communities and causes poverty.

**Q3 a)** El nivel de crimen en mi ciudad es el más bajo de Inglaterra.

**b)** De todos los problemas de la sociedad, la pobreza es **uno de los peores**.

**c)** El nivel de paro / desempleo es **el más alto** de Europa.

**d)** Este año, la campaña de la organización benéfica es **una de las mejores**.

**Q4** Creo que lograr / conseguir la igualdad es el mayor problema de la sociedad actual. Es fácil evitar este problema, pero es importante que luchemos contra el prejuicio. Creo que es la responsabilidad de todos de hacer campaña para la igualdad. Espero que el gobierno escuche y haga algo.

## Page 49 — Contributing to Society

**Q1 a)** One has to recycle to help the environment.

**b) It seems that** some people need more support than others.

**c) One has to** protect the vulnerable / vulnerable people.

**d) It is said that** changing to renewable energy is easy.

**Q2 a)** Siempre intento reutilizar mucho plástico.

**b)** Separaban el vidrio, el plástico y el cartón.

**c)** Organizábamos la basura cada día porque el reciclaje / reciclar es importante.

**d)** Javi convertía sus desperdicios de comida en abono.

**Q3 a)** la gente más pobre

**b)** los afectados

**c)** present subjunctive

Mi tía trabaja para una organización benéfica que cuida de la gente más pobre de todo el mundo. Lucha por los derechos humanos de los afectados o amenazados por el hambre y la guerra. La admiro mucho por ayudarles y espero que un día pueda ayudar también.

# Answers

**Q4** Every Saturday, my friend works as a volunteer / volunteers at a nursing / old people's home. I wouldn't like it because she has to cook, but she loves preparing and serving food to all the people who live there. She has helped others / other people from a young age, and when she's older, she wants to work as a nurse.

## Page 50 — Global Events

**Q1** Sentences **b)** and **c)** should be ticked.
  **a)** El/La atleta estaba enfermo/a antes de los Juegos Olímpicos.
  **b)** Agua potable para todos es lo que quiere el gobierno.
  **c)** El trabajo voluntario será obligatorio en los colegios dentro de diez años.
  **d)** Las organizaciones benéficas están trabajando en condiciones difíciles.
  **e)** Están contentos con la seguridad para el Mundial.

**Q2** **a)** They had started the war without considering / thinking about the consequences.
  **b)** habían muerto — Too many people had already died.
  **c)** Habían perdido — They had lost everything in the earthquake.
  **d)** Habían hablado — They had talked a lot about the World Cup before they went.

**Q3** **a)** **Diego:** La semana pasada, hubo una manifestación en nombre de la igualdad.
  **Elena:** Es una lástima que todavía sea un problema global tan grande.
  **b)** **Paula:** El año que viene / El año próximo, habrá un festival de música internacional en nuestra ciudad / nuestro pueblo.
  **Alexa:** Mucha gente hacía / hizo campaña para tenerlo aquí.
  **c)** **Emma:** La ley cambia / está cambiando para que los hipermercados puedan vender más productos de comercio justo.
  **Chloe:** Sí, oí eso / lo he escuchado. El cambio beneficiará a mucha gente.

**Q4** Starting in (the year) 1909, International Women's Day is celebrated every year on the 8th of March. The day celebrates the social, economic, political and cultural successes / achievements of women. Gender inequality still exists but we hope that a day will arrive / is coming when it won't exist any more / it will cease to exist.

## Pages 51-53 — Mixed Practice

**Q1** **a)** Last year's earthquake left many people without homes / homeless.
  **b)** Due to worldwide campaigns, the rate of deforestation has slowed down.
  **c)** There were some terrible floods which created a lot of poverty.
  **d)** The charity tries / is trying to solve the world's environmental problems.

**Q2** Dormía muy bien porque vivía en el campo y era tranquilo allí. Ahora vivo en la ciudad y hay mucho tráfico por la noche. Intento acostarme temprano pero es difícil dormir a causa de la contaminación / polución acústica. Siempre estoy cansada.

**Q3** **a)** Mi madre nunca come comida basura, pero nunca hace ejercicio tampoco.
  **b)** Él se emborrachaba mucho pero ahora está muy sano y corre cuatro veces por semana.
  **c)** Mi hermana quiere dejar de fumar porque quiere correr un maratón.
  **d)** No podía dormir pero el médico me dio unas pastillas y ya no tengo problemas.

**Q4** **a)** **José:** Do you still work at the charity shop at the weekends?
  **Sami:** Unfortunately, the shop was destroyed by last month's hurricane.
  **b)** **Luisa:** Tomorrow, I'm going to collect / gather / pick up all the plastic from the local park.
  **Toma:** I think it will raise awareness of the problem of plastic.
  **c)** **Katya:** I'm going to buy an electric car. It will be better for the environment.
  **Sofía:** Their development is very important to reduce pollution levels.

**Q5** **a)** Many children suffer problems due to the high levels of pollution.
  **b)** My friend fell and broke her leg when the earthquake destroyed her house / home.
  **c)** Lots of people got / became ill / sick after last year's floods.
  **d)** Some women worry that exhaust fumes harm their babies.
  **e)** It is easy to get sunburnt because the ozone layer is very thin.

**Q6** Hace cinco años, no tenía empleo y estaba sin hogar / "sin techo". Una organización benéfica local me ayudó a encontrar un empleo. Tuve suerte porque la gente que trabajaba allí me dio mucho apoyo. En el futuro, me gustaría / quisiera trabajar como voluntario para ayudar a otros.

**Q7** **a)** **Juan:** El Mundial creará muchos empleos y bajará el desempleo.
  **Nico:** Sin embargo, solamente ayudará de manera temporal / temporalmente. La gente no tendrá empleo cuando termine.
  **b)** **Juan:** Voy a trabajar en un festival de música en agosto. ¿Quieres venir?
  **Nico:** No puedo porque estaré trabajando como voluntario para una organización benéfica para niños.
  **c)** **Juan:** ¿Viste el concierto en México que organizaron aquellos famosos para la organización benéfica?
  **Nico:** Sí, lo vi en la televisión. Di dinero a la organización benéfica después.

Answers

# Answers

**Q8** For people who live in poverty, it can be difficult to lead a healthy life. Often, food containing lots of sugar or salt is cheaper than healthier options. That means that it is difficult for people with little money to get the nourishment they need from their food.

**Q9** The government wants people to cycle more and walk instead of driving. It would be better for the environment. It seems good to me / I think it's good that the government is thinking about it, but I don't think it's the most important problem. We should give more help to those who need it in our society.

**Q10 a) Kris:** ¿Quieres probar un trozo de este pastel de chocolate?
**Coral:** Me encantaría pero ya no puedo comer chocolate. He descubierto que soy alérgica a la leche.
**b) Kris:** ¿Has tenido que cambiar tu dieta?
**Coral:** Sí, pero ahora lo encuentro más fácil comer más saludablemente / sanamente.
**c) Kris:** Está bien / Excelente, ¿ahora tienes más energía?
**Coral:** Sí, y me siento más saludable / sana.

**Q11 a)** It is important that we reduce emissions. We should use more renewable energy in our society, for example using electric / the use of electricity to power cars.
**b)** However, the technology is still quite expensive which excludes lots of people. It doesn't seem (to me) to be accessible to all parts of society.

**Q12** Acaba de abrir una tienda de comida nueva cerca de mi casa. En la tienda, hay envases / contenedores grandes de comida. La gente puede usarlos para llenar sus propios botes y bolsas. También la tienda cree en dar oportunidades justas a la gente. Se emplea a mucha gente que ha tenido dificultades en encontrar empleos a causa de sus incapacidades.

## Section 6 — Travel and Tourism

### Page 54 — Where to Go

**Q1 a)** I went on holiday to France.
**b)** irás — Where will you go next year?
**c)** Prefieren, ir — They prefer to go on holiday abroad.
**d)** Nos quedaremos — We will stay in Madrid for a few nights.

**Q2 a)** ¿Cuándo vais a regresar / volver a Grecia?
**b)** ¿**Adónde** queréis ir de vacaciones este año?
**c)** ¿**Cuántos** días os quedasteis en los Estados Unidos?
**d)** ¿**Cuál** es tu país preferido?

**Q3 a)** Last year he / she spent time in Scotland with his / her stepfather.
**b)** I'm going to stay in the south of Germany this summer.
**c)** They want to go back to Italy next July to see their friends.

**d)** In the future, I'd like to visit my family in Wales.

**Q4** Quisiera / Me gustaría ir al extranjero cada año, pero es muy caro. Tenemos suerte porque mis abuelos viven en España, por eso / así que podemos quedarnos con ellos.

**Q5 a) Alma:** Javier, are you going on holiday with your parents? They've told me that they're going to Japan.
**Javier:** Yes, we're going for two weeks and we want to visit Tokyo.
**b) Alma:** You're so lucky / How lucky! I will go to Japan next year with my girlfriend.
**Javier:** What would you want to do there? I'm really looking forward to going to Japan.
**c) Alma:** I want to go to the museums in Tokyo. I'm interested in Japanese culture.
**Javier:** I'll tell you all about our trip when we get back.

## Page 55 — Accommodation

**Q1 a)** Este hotel tiene las instalaciones excelentes.
**b)** big — Busco / Estoy buscando alojamiento con una piscina grande.
**c)** another — Hay otro hotel con aire acondicionado.
**d)** clean — La pensión siempre tiene sábanas limpias.

**Q2 a)** If there are still rooms available in the boarding house, I would like a double bedroom.
**b)** Tomorrow we could stay at the youth hostel.
**c)** I think that half board would be best.
**d)** You should phone / call the hotel to make the reservation.

**Q3 a)** Los albergues juveniles son más interesantes que los hoteles.
**b)** Es **más caro** quedarse en un hotel de lujo.
**c)** El camping es **tan divertido como** hacer un crucero.
**d)** Una tienda es **menos cómoda que** un parador.
**e)** Esta habitación es **más moderna que** esa / aquella.

**Q4** When we go on holiday, we usually go camping. I think that it's better than staying in a hotel because campsites cost much less than hotels and usually have really good facilities. For example, a campsite I visited last year had a pool and it was next to the beach.

## Page 56 — Getting Ready

**Q1 a)** Jo quise / quería hacer una reserva / reservación.
**b)** The room — La habitación tiene vistas al mar.
**c)** We — Quisiéramos un mapa de la ciudad.
**d)** the hotel — ¿Tendrá el hotel algunas habitaciones individuales disponibles?

**Q2 a)** Para mí, es importante aprender la lengua local antes de viajar al extranjero.
**b)** No quiero visitar el museo sin él.
**c)** Gabriel, ¿vas a llevar tu guía contigo?

# Answers

**Q3** **a)** It's important that you pack your suitcase a few days before your journey.
**b)** tenga — I hope that the state-owned hotel has rooms with views of the mountains.
**c)** lleguen — I'm going to speak to them when they arrive at the hotel.
**d)** sea — I don't believe that Las Alas de Hada is the best hotel in the city.

**Q4** I love taking photos when I visit new places. Last year I went to India and a monkey stole my camera. I need to buy a new one before I go to Africa in August.

**Q5** **a) Inma:** ¿Tienes muchas ganas de ir de vacaciones?
**Paula:** Sí, pero tengo mil cosas que hacer antes de irme.
**b) Inma:** ¿Qué tienes que hacer? Todavía tienes mucho tiempo.
**Paula:** Hay que / Necesito solicitar un nuevo pasaporte.
**c) Inma:** Deberías organizarlo pronto. Tuve que esperar dos meses por el mío.
**Paula:** Lo haré por la mañana.

## Page 57 — Getting There

**Q1** **a)** La estación de servicio estaba lejos.
**b)** here — ¿Hay una estación de(l) metro por aquí?
**c)** everywhere — A Jo le gusta conducir por todas partes.
**d)** there — Viajaron allí / allá en avión.

**Q2** **a)** His / her / their friends prefer to travel by boat.
**b)** future — The train to Barcelona will depart from platform six.
**c)** preterite — I bought a return ticket to Madrid.
**d)** perfect — We've rented the car for two weeks.

**Q3** **a)** muy tarde
**b)** tardó tres horas
**c)** future
Mi vuelo llegó muy tarde al aeropuerto. El conductor del autobús dijo que había un atasco en la autopista. Decidí coger el tren. Estaba muy concurrido y el viaje tardó tres horas. La próxima vez, alquilaré un coche.

**Q4** After arriving at the station more than twenty minutes late, I was worried about arriving late for the meeting. I was on the corner of the street next to the station when I heard my name. I saw my colleague / friend, Jenny, who had booked a taxi to take her to the meeting. I went with her and we arrived on time.

## Pages 58-59 — What to Do

**Q1** **a)** ¿Qué te gusta hacer cuando vas de vacaciones?
**b)** visiting — A mi madre le gusta visitar el parque temático.
**c)** see — Puedes ver más de la ciudad a pie.
**d)** going — Me encanta ir a la playa.

**Q2** **a)** el — Juan would swim in the sea every day but the water is cold.

**b)** las, la — I want to see the photos in the art gallery.
**c)** el, el — I love to spend the day sunbathing.
**d)** el, el — We bought the souvenir at the theme park.

**Q3** **a)** Estamos pensando en ir a montar a caballo / hacer equitación.
**b)** Mis padres **están sacando** fotos del castillo.
**c)** **Estoy mandando / enviando** una postal a mi madre.
**d)** ¿**Estás / Estáis comprando** un billete antes de viajar?

**Q4** intentamos / estamos intentando; le gusta el surf; le encanta visitar; no me importa mucho.

**Q5** **a)** I did lots of water sports when I was in Malaga.
**b)** conocimos — We are going to play basketball with the boys from England who we met yesterday.
**c)** Tuvieron — They were too scared to do adventure sports.
**d)** Viste — Did you see a show when you were in London?
**e)** prometió — My sister promised me that we could go mountain climbing.

**Q6** **a)** No estaba nadie en el museo.
**b)** **No compramos nunca** recuerdos.
**c)** **No hay nada** más que hacer.
**d)** **No queda ninguna plaza** en la excursión.

**Q7** **a) Claudia:** Hello, Pedro. Are you enjoying your holidays?
**Pedro:** Yes. Today I went to the monument, and tomorrow I'm going to look at the castle ruins. Do you want to come with me?
**b) Claudia:** I can't. I already have plans. I'm going shopping to look for souvenirs.
**Pedro:** What time are you going? Do you want to have lunch together? I will be eating at two.
**c) Claudia:** Yes, I'd love to. I want to try the local food / food from this region. It looks delicious.
**Pedro:** Yes, I'm looking forward to trying the sweets!

**Q8** My ideal holiday would be in a country where you can ski in the mornings and relax on the beach in the afternoons. I've heard that this is possible in North America and in parts of Spain. For me, it's more fun to do something active than sunbathe all day.

## Page 60 — Practical Stuff

**Q1** **a)** Por favor ¿(usted) me puede ayudar?
**b)** ¿Ha perdido (usted) el monedero?
**c)** ¿Tiene (usted) mapa que puedo pedir prestado?
**d)** ¿Puede (usted) llevarme al garaje para recoger mi coche?
**e)** ¿Ha visto (usted) una comisaría cerca de aquí?
**f)** ¿Sabe (usted) dónde puedo confirmar mi billete?

**Q2** **a)** We have missed the train.
**b)** ha dejado — She has left her suitcase on the tram.

# Answers

c) **han robado** — They have stolen my mobile phone.

d) **Has encontrado** — Have you found your ticket?

**Q3** a) **Manni:** What happened to your arm?
**Laura:** I had a car crash on holiday and I broke it.

b) **Greg:** Our holiday was terrible. The hotel was really dirty.
**Paul:** What a shame! You should complain to the company.

c) **Victor:** Excuse me, waitress, do you have a table for two available?
**Sophie:** Yes, but there is a waiting time of one hour. Do you want to wait?

**Q4** En abril, fuimos de vacaciones a España. Fuimos en barco desde Portsmouth a Santander, porque queríamos llevar nuestro coche. Llegamos a España en hora punta, y las carreteras estaban muy concurridas. Alguien nos intentó adelantar / intentó adelantarnos y mi padre tuvo que frenar rápidamente. Tuvimos suerte porque ¡no hubo (ningún) accidente!

## Pages 61-63 — Mixed Practice

**Q1** a) Hacía mucho calor en España, entonces practicábamos deportes acuáticos todos los días.

b) Cuando fue a Gales, Emily tenía demasiado miedo para montar a caballo / hacer equitación.

c) Me gustaría probar el esquí cuando visite Francia el año que viene / el año próximo.

d) Cuando fue a Londres, vio mucho de la ciudad y visitó muchos monumentos.

e) Alquilé un coche cuando fui a Dinamarca, así que tuve que llevar mi carnet de conducir conmigo.

f) Tiene muchas ganas de probar la comida local cuando vaya a Pakistán.

**Q2** a) Annika couldn't go to the theme park because she had forgotten her purse.

b) We were lucky because there weren't (any) traffic jams on the motorway.

c) He / she can't go on holiday this year because his / her mother has broken her leg.

d) Unfortunately, the hotel made a mistake and cancelled our reservation.

e) The waitress gave us a discount on our bill because we had lots of problems.

**Q3** When I go on holiday, I walk around the city every day. What I like doing is going to castle ruins. This year I'm going to Bilbao, and I'm going to visit one of the oldest castles in Spain. I've bought a new camera to take lots of photos.

**Q4** Me encantaría ir de vacaciones al extranjero, pero es demasiado caro. Sin embargo, hay muchas actividades divertidas que se puede hacer aquí en el Reino Unido. Me gusta ir de camping, pero mi saco de dormir no es muy cómodo. Cuando sea mayor, espero que tenga bastante dinero para quedarme en hoteles.

**Q5** a) **Sonia:** Have you been to Holland? I will go by boat from Hull in the summer.
**Tony:** Yes, I went there a few years ago. Which part are you going to?

b) **Sonia:** We're going to Amsterdam. We're staying for three nights in total.
**Tony:** I've visited Amsterdam and there are lots of museums and art galleries.

c) **Sonia:** I'm not interested in going to museums or galleries. What else is there to do?
**Tony:** You could rent a bicycle. It's a good way to see the city.

**Q6** a) No pasarán mucho tiempo en el albergue juvenil porque hay muchas cosas que hacer.

b) Quiero comer en restaurantes locales, así que sería mejor quedarnos en media pensión.

c) Queremos un hotel con una piscina para que los niños puedan nadar.

d) Prefiero quedarme en habitaciones de hoteles con balcón con una vista al mar.

e) No le gusta viajar en avión, por eso / así que normalmente conduce a Portugal.

**Q7** Unfortunately, my return journey to England last week was a disaster. I got lost on the way to the airport and had to ask for directions several times. Upon arriving late at the airport, I discovered that my flight was cancelled. Next time, I'll go by boat. It will be much easier than flying!

**Q8** El año pasado, pasé las vacaciones viajando por Europa en tren. Fue un viaje fantástico porque me interesa mucho el ferrocarril. Las vistas a las sierras del tren eran bonitas. La única dificultad fue que no hablo ni francés ni alemán, así que a veces era difícil encontrar el andén para el próximo tren.

**Q9** a) We would like to stay in Berlin, but none of the hotels have rooms available.

b) It will be really hot in Australia, so I'll book a room with air conditioning.

c) The hotel is famous for its food, and for this reason I chose to stay full board.

**Q10** a) **Kyle:** Hola, quiero / quisiera reservar una habitación de hotel para mis vacaciones. ¿Me puede ayudar?
**José:** Por supuesto. ¿Adónde quiere ir?

b) **Kyle:** Quiero ir a un país caluroso. Me encantaría relajarme al lado de la piscina todo el día.
**José:** Hay muchos hoteles con piscinas grandes en Italia. ¿Le gustaría ir allí?

# Answers

c) **Kyle:** Sí, nunca he ido a Italia.
**José:** He encontrado un hotel cerca de Roma con una habitación disponible. Haré una reserva / reservación para usted / Le haré una reserva / reservación.

**Q11** Durante mi año libre viajé a muchos países, pero nunca visité América del Sur / Sudamérica. Cuando sea mayor, me gustaría ir a Perú. Me quedaría con mi amiga que vive en Lima. Me gustaría visitarla porque no la veo desde hace dos años.

**Q12** Last year I went to New Zealand. I stayed in youth hostels and it was really fun. I travelled by public transport but I found it difficult because the buses always arrived late. Next time, I will rent a car to visit more remote places. There are still lots of places (left) for me to visit.

## Section 7 — Current & Future Study and Employment

### Pages 64-65 — School Life

**Q1** a) Tienen educación física antes de la comida / del almuerzo, a la una.
b) Tomo / Como una merienda por / durante la tarde a las dos y media.
c) Tenemos recreo desde las diez y media hasta las once menos cuarto.
d) El colegio / instituto público termina a las tres y veinticinco.
e) Las nueve y diez es demasiado temprano para la clase de matemáticas.

**Q2** a) I hate it because it is boring and I don't get good marks.
b) la — Last Monday, I left it on the bus.
c) me — They always help me with my homework.
d) la — They decorated it with Spanish flags and maps of the country.

**Q3** a) ✓ — You have to / One has to arrive on time.
b) ✓ — The correct uniform should be worn.
c) x — It's prohibited to use mobile phones in school.
d) x — You / One cannot talk in the library.
e) ✓ — Show respect to others.

**Q4** el acoso; comprensivos; te sientes amenazado/a; no tengas miedo; te puede ayudar / puede ayudarte.

**Q5** a) El comedor es más nuevo que las aulas.
b) El colegio / instituto religioso es **tan grande como** el colegio / instituto privado.
c) Los vestuarios son **más ruidosos que** la biblioteca.
d) Hoy, el taller está **tan frío como** el gimnasio.

**Q6** The following verbs should be circled: habíamos hecho, había roto.
The following verbs should be underlined: he perdido, ha comprado.
a) Olivia and Tom had forgotten their geography books.

b) José and I hadn't done the homework for our Latin class / our Latin homework.
c) I have lost my pen and I don't have another for tomorrow's exam.
d) Jaime has bought coloured pencils for his art class.
e) We couldn't do the activity because the interactive / smart board had broken.

**Q7** Durante el recreo, solemos charlar, pero ayer fuimos a la biblioteca para terminar nuestros deberes de matemáticas. A veces vamos a la cantina. En el verano, jugamos al fútbol en el campo o nos relajamos en el patio, pero en el invierno preferimos quedarnos en el aula.

**Q8** a) **Pablo:** I'm really stressed about the exams. My parents want me to get good grades.
**Ana:** I've read an article about how to reduce stress levels during exams.
b) **Pablo:** Did you learn anything useful?
**Ana:** I read that it is important to relax.
c) **Pablo:** It's more difficult than it seems. I have to revise a lot so that I don't fail.
**Ana:** You don't have to worry. I know that you're going to pass.

### Page 66 — School Events

**Q1** a) Tenemos demasiadas pruebas en clase.
b) La orquesta hace **muchos** espectáculos.
c) Solo quedan **pocos** días del año escolar.
d) Hay **tantos** anuncios en el periódico del colegio.

**Q2** a) All classes will be cancelled on Tuesday.
b) será mostrado — The documentary will be shown at film club on Thursday.
c) será organizada — The school trip will be organised by the students.
d) será cambiado — Choir practice will be changed from Monday to Wednesday.

**Q3** a) preterite
b) una buena oportunidad / una oportunidad buena
c) nunca / jamás
Cada año hay un viaje al extranjero con el departamento de idiomas. El año pasado fuimos a España y fue una buena oportunidad para practicar el español. El año que viene / El año próximo, los/las profesores/as quieren visitar Francia. No he visitado Francia nunca antes.

**Q4** Parents' evening will take place in October. After the last parents' evening, my parents got angry because my teachers said that I didn't make an effort. Since then I've paid attention during lessons / classes. Last Thursday, we had a prize-giving (ceremony), and I won a prize. My parents are very proud of me.

### Page 67 — Education Post-16

**Q1** a) After my A-levels, I would like to take a gap year.
b) encantaría — I would love to work for a few months to earn money.

# Answers

c) viajaría — In an ideal world, I would travel around Europe with a friend.

d) estudiaría — If I had the money, I would study law at university.

**Q2**
a) Si suspendo mis exámenes, intentaré de nuevo el año que viene / el año próximo.

b) Estudiaré para ser programador/a si saco buenas notas en la informática.

c) Si apruebo el examen de español, lo estudiaré en el bachillerato.

d) Mis padres se enfadarán conmigo si no me esfuerzo.

**Q3**
a) **Elías:** ¿Qué harás cuando termines tus estudios?
**Kiara:** No sé si haré un aprendizaje o continuaré con mis estudios en el colegio.

b) **Elías:** ¿Sabes qué tipo de trabajo te gustaría hacer en el futuro?
**Kiara:** Me gustaría ser jardinera. Quiero trabajar al aire libre.

c) **Elías:** Sería útil hacer una experiencia laboral.
**Kiara:** Pienso que eso es una buena idea.

**Q4** Last year I did my work experience in a car factory. I liked it because I want to become an engineer and the work was interesting. However, the factory closed two months ago so I can't return / go back to work there when I finish my studies. It's a shame because it would have been my ideal job.

## Page 68 — Languages for the Future

**Q1**
a) Creo que los/las profesores/as de lenguas / idiomas hacen un trabajo importante.

b) Dudo que el latín sea útil ahora.

c) Pienso que los intérpretes tienen un trabajo interesante.

d) No creo / pienso que la gente necesite aprender lenguas / idiomas.

**Q2**
a) advantageous
b) skills
c) the world today
Learning languages is advantageous in today's society. Not only do they help you improve your communication skills, languages also give you the opportunity to get to know / meet new people, and see the world from another perspective. To be able to communicate in other languages is important in the world today.

**Q3** Trabajo en una oficina de turismo y sé hablar varias lenguas / varios idiomas diferentes. Los turistas lo encuentran muy útil cuando puedo explicarles algo en su propia lengua / propio idioma. En mi opinión, es importante que todo el mundo aprenda una lengua / un idioma diferente.

**Q4**
a) **Keri:** What do you want to do when you're older?
**Sam:** I want to work in business, so I'm learning Japanese.

b) **Keri:** I think that German would be more useful.
**Sam:** Yes, but I would like to live in Japan in the future.

c) **Keri:** I'd like a job that uses my language skills.
**Sam:** Think about being a translator. You can earn money by translating documents.

## Page 69 — Applying for Jobs

**Q1**
a) self-confident — Necesitamos a empleados responsables y seguros de sí mismos.

b) good, organised — Se le da bien su trabajo porque es organizado.

c) nasty — Quiero cambiar mi trabajo porque el jefe / la jefa es tacaño/a.

d) successful, hard-working — Ella tiene éxito porque es trabajadora.

**Q2**
a) It is easier to get a job if you have experience.

b) puede — If your job is badly paid, you can find a new one.

c) necesita — You need to write an application letter.

d) deben — You should do an apprenticeship in the summer.

**Q3** Waiters or waitresses wanted to work in a busy café in the city centre. Friendly employees needed. Punctuality is also important, and it's not necessary to have experience. If you are interested, come to the café with your application letter.

**Q4**
a) **Sara:** Hola, he visto su anuncio de trabajo y quisiera solicitar el puesto de electricista.
**Nico:** Vale, ¿qué habilidades relevantes tiene usted?

b) **Sara:** Acabo de terminar una calificación de electricista. También tengo experiencia de trabajar en la empresa de mi tío.
**Nico:** Muy bien. Creo que la experiencia es importante. La llamaré después de entrevistar a los otros candidatos.

## Page 70 — Career Choices and Ambitions

**Q1**
a) My mum wants me to have a job that pays well.

b) encuentres — It's important that you find a job that you like.

c) sepa — They need someone who knows French and Italian.

d) sea — I hope that she is happy in her new job.

**Q2**
a) Quiero ser dentista porque puedes / se puede ganar mucho dinero.

b) Será una buena profesora porque le gusta trabajar con los niños.

c) Ser médico/a es difícil porque hay mucha presión.

d) Le encanta el arte dramático y sueña con llegar a ser un actor famoso.

**Q3**
a) She has a creative personality and would like to work as a designer.

b) If you don't wish to work in an office, you could learn to be a brick-layer.

c) I would love to be a firefighter because I want to do something useful.

**Q4** Helena espera llegar a ser militar / soldado cuando sea mayor. No es una carrera fácil, pero se puede viajar y ayudar a otra gente. Hay que ser muy activo y trabajador para triunfar.

# Answers

**Q5** I have a part-time job in a hairdresser's opposite my house. I've worked there for a year and a half. I love it because the people are nice, but the worst thing is that I have to get up early on Saturdays. I would like to be a hairdresser in the future and have my own business.

## Pages 71-73 — Mixed Practice

**Q1 a)** Antes de empezar un título / una licenciatura de derecho, hay que / tienes que estudiarlo en el bachillerato.
**b)** (Ella) va a hacer un aprendizaje con un/a electricista local.
**c)** Mi profesor/a organizó mi experiencia laboral en una escuela primaria.
**d)** Voy a estudiar arte porque quiero llegar a ser pintor/a.
**e)** (A ella) le gustan las matemáticas, así que va a trabajar como cajera en un banco.
**f)** Si quieres ser enfermero/a, tienes que sacar buenas notas en las ciencias.

**Q2** We are looking for someone older than 16 / Someone older than 16 is needed to help in a beauty salon. Responsibilities will include: helping customers, answering the phone, organising appointments and preparing treatments. You must be punctual and hard-working. Those interested should fill out the application (form) and send it by email.

**Q3 a)** At Christmas, our choir is going to sing in the school hall.
**b)** My parents gave me permission to go on the geography trip on Wednesday.
**c)** If you make a donation tomorrow, you won't have to wear (your) uniform.
**d)** They are going to sell biscuits in the (school) canteen to support a local charity.

**Q4** Voy al sur de Alemania pronto para trabajar como canguro. Todavía no he conocido a la familia así que estoy un poco nerviosa. Organicé este trabajo a través de una empresa que un/una amigo/a ha utilizado. Espero tener muchas oportunidades para mejorar mi alemán antes de estudiarlo en la universidad el año que viene / el año próximo.

**Q5 a)** I went to London and when I was there, I organised some work experience.
**b)** I met a local civil servant and we spoke / were speaking in English throughout / for the interview.
**c)** I studied Portuguese and German at university and that impressed him. He offered me the job.
**d)** I am going to work in the Spanish embassy and use my knowledge of various / several languages.

**Q6** Last week some people came to school and they talked / spoke to us about their jobs. A chef did / gave a demonstration on Tuesday. He showed us how to prepare a paella, and gave / told us information about his profession / career. I still don't know what I want to do in the future. I'm going to look into / for career options on the internet / online.

**Q7 a) Mateo:** Me encantaría tomar un año libre y viajar a Latinoamérica. Me gustaría trabajar como voluntario con una organización benéfica.
**b) Leon:** He visto un anuncio para enfermeros para trabajar en un hospital local. Buscan a gente que tenga un título / una licenciatura de biología. Voy a solicitar el puesto.
**c) Sara:** Cuando sea mayor, quiero ser carnicera, por eso hago un aprendizaje con una empresa / compañía local. En el futuro, quiero ser la jefa de mi propia empresa / compañía.

**Q8** El acoso escolar me molesta porque es muy injusto. Es un gran problema en los institutos. En el futuro quiero ser consejero/a que ayuda a las víctimas del acoso. Voy a estudiar psicología en la universidad. Necesitaré / Tendré que ser paciente y escuchar bien a otras personas.

**Q9 a)** El año pasado sentí mucha presión en el colegio / instituto. Me preocupaba suspender los exámenes. Mis profesores/as me dieron mucho apoyo y los aprobé.
**b)** Pienso que el francés es aburrido, así que a menudo estoy ausente de / falto a las clases. Mi madre quiere que vaya a clase. Piensa que aprender una lengua es importante.
**c)** Voy a un colegio / instituto religioso, y los estudios religiosos son obligatorios. Preferiría ir a un colegio / instituto público, porque los alumnos tienen más variedad en las asignaturas que estudian.

**Q10** Dear Miss García, I read your advert that a journalist is wanted / you're looking for a journalist. I would like to apply for the position. I have studied journalism for three years and I passed the final exams at university with excellent results. I don't believe that there is a more perfect candidate because I have the experience, enthusiasm and skill required for this job. Yours sincerely. Clara Smith.

**Q11 a) Ana:** I'm thinking about joining the army. Is it true that your dad is a soldier?
**Karl:** He was a soldier many years ago, but now he is a policeman.
**b) Kai:** Does your brother still want to be a writer? He used to be / was interested in what was happening in the world.
**Luc:** Yes, that's his aim. He has found a job with the local newspaper.
**c) Tina:** My mum wants me to be a nurse like her but I want to travel.
**Ali:** You could work as a nurse in the military / armed forces. It would be very varied and you would work in other countries.